Karen Calhoun
John J. Riemer
Editors

CORC:
New Tools and Possibilities
for Cooperative Electronic
Resource Description

CORC: New Tools and Possibilities for Cooperative Electronic Resource Description has been co-published simultaneously as *Journal of Internet Cataloging,* Volume 4, Numbers 1/2 2001.

Pre-publication
REVIEWS,
COMMENTARIES,
EVALUATIONS . . .

"**P**rovides an astute balance of the theoretical with the practical, of the manager's point of view with the specialist's. All of the chapters are well written and offer thought-provoking insights. I highly recommend this book for any individual or institution trying to bring order to the chaos and to take positive steps to building a real digital library."

Carol G. Hixson, MS
Head, Catalog Department
University of Oregon;
Chair, PCC Standing Committee
on Training

CORC:
New Tools and Possibilities for Cooperative Electronic Resource Description

CORC: New Tools and Possibilities for Cooperative Electronic Resource Description has been co-published simultaneously as *Journal of Internet Cataloging,* Volume 4, Numbers 1/2 2001.

The *Journal of Internet Cataloging* Monographic "Separates"

Below is a list of "separates," which in serials librarianship means a special issue simultaneously published as a special journal issue or double-issue *and* as a "separate" hardbound monograph. (This is a format which we also call a "DocuSerial.")

"Separates" are published because specialized libraries or professionals may wish to purchase a specific thematic issue by itself in a format which can be separately cataloged and shelved, as opposed to purchasing the journal on an on-going basis. Faculty members may also more easily consider a "separate" for classroom adoption.

"Separates" are carefully classified separately with the major book jobbers so that the journal tie-in can be noted on new book order slips to avoid duplicate purchasing.

You may wish to visit Haworth's website at . . .

http://www.HaworthPress.com

. . . to search our online catalog for complete tables of contents of these separates and related publications.

You may also call 1-800-HAWORTH (outside US/Canada: 607-722-5857), or Fax 1-800-895-0582 (outside US/Canada: 607-771-0012), or e-mail at:

getinfo@haworthpressinc.com

CORC: New Tools and Possibilities for Cooperative Electronic Resource Description, edited by Karen Calhoun, MS, MBA, and John J. Riemer, MLS (Vol. 4, No. 1/2, 2001). *Examines the nuts-and-bolts practical matters of making a cataloging system work in the Internet environment, where information objects are electronic, transient, and numerous.*

Metadata and Organizing Educational Resources on the Internet, edited by Jane Greenberg, PhD (Vol. 3, No. 1/2/3, 2000). *"A timely and essential reference. . . . A compilation of important issues and views . . . provides the reader with a balanced and practical presentation of empirical case studies and theoretical elaboration." (John Mason, Co-Chair, Dublin Core Education Working Group, and Technical Director, Education, Au LTD [Education Network Australia])*

Internet Searching and Indexing: The Subject Approach, edited by Alan R. Thomas, MA, and James R. Shearer, MA (Vol. 2, No. 3/4, 2000). *This handy guide examines the tools and procedures available now and for the future that will help librarians, students, and patrons search the Internet more systematical, and also discusses how Internet pages can be modified to facilitate easier and efficient searches.*

CORC:
New Tools and Possibilities for Cooperative Electronic Resource Description

Karen Calhoun
John J. Riemer
Editors

CORC: New Tools and Possibilities for Cooperative Electronic Resource Description has been co-published simultaneously as *Journal of Internet Cataloging,* Volume 4, Numbers 1/2 2001.

The Haworth Information Press
An Imprint of
The Haworth Press, Inc.
New York • London • Oxford

Published by

The Haworth Information Press, 10 Alice Street, Binghamton, NY 13904-1580 USA

The Haworth Information Press is an imprint of The Haworth Press, Inc., 10 Alice Street, Binghamton, NY 13904-1580 USA.

CORC: New Tools and Possibilities for Cooperative Electronic Resource Description has been co-published simultaneously as *Journal of Internet Cataloging,* Volume 4, Numbers 1/2 2001.

The development, preparation, and publication of this work has been undertaken with great care. However, the publisher, employees, editors, and agents of The Haworth Press and all imprints of The Haworth Press, Inc., including The Haworth Medical Press® and Pharmaceutical Products Press®, are not responsible for any errors contained herein or for consequences that may ensue from use of materials or information contained in this work. Opinions expressed by the author(s) are not necessarily those of The Haworth Press, Inc.

Cover design by Thomas J. Mayshock Jr.

Library of Congress Cataloging-in-Publication Data

CORC : new tools and possibilities for cooperative electronic resource description / Karen Calhoun, John J. Riemer, editors.
     p. cm.
    "Co-published simultaneously as Journal of internet cataloging, volume 4, numbers 1/2, 2001."
    ISBN 0-7890-1304-5 (alk. paper)–ISBN 0-7890-1305-3 (alk. paper)
    1. OCLC. CORC. 2. Cataloging of computer network resources. 3. Dublin Core. 4. Cataloging, Cooperative. I. Calhoun, Karen. II. Riemer, John J. III. Journal of Internet cataloging.
Z695.24 .C67 2000
025.3'44–dc21   00-050551

Indexing, Abstracting & Website/Internet Coverage

This section provides you with a list of major indexing & abstracting services. That is to say, each service began covering this periodical during the year noted in the right column. Most Websites which are listed below have indicated that they will either post, disseminate, compile, archive, cite or alert their own Website users with research-based content from this work. (This list is as current as the copyright date of this publication.)

(continued)

Special Bibliographic Notes related to special journal issues (separates) and indexing/abstracting:

- indexing/abstracting services in this list will also cover material in any "separate" that is co-published simultaneously with Haworth's special thematic journal issue or DocuSerial. Indexing/abstracting usually covers material at the article/chapter level.
- monographic co-editions are intended for either non-subscribers or libraries which intend to purchase a second copy for their circulating collections.
- monographic co-editions are reported to all jobbers/wholesalers/approval plans. The source journal is listed as the "series" to assist the prevention of duplicate purchasing in the same manner utilized for books-in-series.
- to facilitate user/access services all indexing/abstracting services are encouraged to utilize the co-indexing entry note indicated at the bottom of the first page of each article/chapter/contribution.
- this is intended to assist a library user of any reference tool (whether print, electronic, online, or CD-ROM) to locate the monographic version if the library has purchased this version but not a subscription to the source journal.
- individual articles/chapters in any Haworth publication are also available through the Haworth Document Delivery Service (HDDS).

CORC:
New Tools and Possibilities for Cooperative Electronic Resource Description

CONTENTS

ABOUT THE EDITORS

Karen Calhoun, MS, MBA, is Director of Central Technical Services at Cornell University Library. She leads Cornell's participation in the CORC project, plays a key role in the organization of the library's networked resources and services, and is a frequent speaker and author on technical services in the digital library. Karen chairs the Program for Cooperative Cataloging (PCC) Standing Committee on Automation. Previously she held positions at OCLC and the University of Oregon.

John J. Riemer, MLS, is the GALILEO CORC Representative in the state of Georgia and Assistant Head of Cataloging at the University of Georgia. He has organized training for and helped to coordinate half a dozen metadata projects. For over ten years he served as Head of Serials Cataloging and represented the library on the CONSER Operations Committee. Previously he held positions at the University of California, Los Angeles.

Hold fast to dreams,
For if dreams die,
Life is a broken-winged bird
That cannot fly.

–Langston Hughes

Preface

This volume, co-published as a special issue of the *Journal of Internet Cataloging*, is special indeed. As the title implies, *CORC: New Tools and Possibilities for Cooperative Electronic Resource Description* documents the issues–technological, standards, economic, and organizational–involved in creating a new cataloging system for electronic resources. It also testifies to the notion that in any endeavor involving people, information and technology, the "people" part is most important.

The Cooperative Online Resource Catalog (CORC) began as a research project in the OCLC Office of Research, which is one of the world's leading centers devoted exclusively to the challenges facing libraries in a rapidly changing information technology environment. Since its founding in 1978, the Office has investigated trends in technology and library practice to identify technical advances that will enhance the value of library services and improve the productivity of librarians and library users. The CORC Project grew out of work OCLC research scientists were doing in metadata, linked authority control, the Web version of the Dewey Decimal Classification, and Mantis software and other automated tools for finding, harvesting and classifying electronic resources. CORC is both a computer system and a collaborative effort among the world's libraries.

In January 1999, CORC came online. St. Joseph's County (Indiana) Public Library was the first institution to catalog on CORC. At this writing, more than 350 libraries are now participating, including the Library of Congress and the U.S. Government Printing Office. Approximately 58 percent of participants are academic libraries; 9 percent are public libraries; and 19 percent are government libraries. Thirteen percent of the participants are outside the United States. The pioneering libraries that have participated in the initial, founding phase of CORC have made valuable contributions to its ongoing development. Participants have held meetings at OCLC and at library conferences, where they provide feedback for both practicing librarians and OCLC system developers.

[Haworth co-indexing entry note]: "Preface." Jordan, Jay. Co-published simultaneously in *Journal of Internet Cataloging* (The Haworth Information Press, an imprint of The Haworth Press, Inc.) Vol. 4, No. 1/2, 2001, pp. xix-xx; and: *CORC: New Tools and Possibilities for Cooperative Electronic Resource Description* (ed: Karen Calhoun, and John J. Riemer) The Haworth Information Press, an imprint of The Haworth Press, Inc., 2001, pp. xv-xvi. Single or multiple copies of this article are available for a fee from The Haworth Document Delivery Service [1-800-342-9678, 9:00 a.m. - 5:00 p.m. (EST). E-mail address: getinfo@haworthpressinc.com].

xv

Indeed, one of the more interesting, and as yet untold, aspects of CORC is the new, concurrent engineering approach that information scientists at OCLC have used to take the system from a research project to an operational service. It has been estimated that one Web year is worth seven traditional development years. At OCLC, we are tracking our CORC development process in Web years. We are using cross-organizational teams. We have re-engineered our development processes for quicker turnaround without compromising quality. And most important, we have worked closely with current CORC users. In some cases, we have been able to install an enhancement suggested by a user within 24 hours.

At this writing, OCLC plans to launch CORC as an operational service later in 2000. CORC will evolve into a general-purpose, Web-based cataloging service and will be a key component of future OCLC Web-based services.

The contributing authors in this volume are engaged in important work. They are dealing with the nuts-and-bolts, practical matters of making a cataloging system work in an environment whose information objects are electronic, transient and numerous. They are also helping to define the future of librarianship and information access at a time when the World Wide Web is transforming not only commerce, but education and communications, indeed, society itself.

Ultimately, CORC is more than tool sets and technological platforms. It is the story of people and libraries working together to advance research, scholarship and education. I would like to thank the authors and the staffs of the 340 institutions who have elected to participate in the founding phase of CORC. They are true pioneers, and they are carrying the spirit of library cooperation into an exciting new era.

Jay Jordan, OCLC
President and CEO

Introduction

Karen Calhoun
John J. Riemer

In the present fast-paced environment, continual innovation in library operations and services is not optional. This volume presents the thoughts and experiences of a group of innovators seeking new ways for libraries to excel. They are
experimenting with CORC (the Cooperative Online Resource Catalog), a
groundbreaking initiative of several hundred libraries and the OCLC Office of
Research, which seeks no less than bringing order to digital chaos, using the
principles of librarianship.

Since their early history, libraries have woven themselves into the fabric of
society. Today, the fabric of society includes the astonishing, revolutionary
threads of the Internet and World Wide Web. The successful libraries and
librarians of the future will be those that step up to the challenge of taking a
leading role in the digital age and that relentlessly build upon past and present
achievements. Often, the pursuit of enduring excellence requires sweeping
away the wisdom of the past and starting anew, learning what works through
experimentation, trial and error, and opportunism.

CORC offers librarians an unparalleled opportunity to innovate. It places
in the hands of librarians everywhere the transformative power of new
technology and standards. The fourteen articles in this volume all tell stories
of new ideas, discoveries, and insights gained by being part of the CORC
project. They represent the perspectives not only of CORC founders, researchers, developers, and observers, but also of library managers and practitioners who are applying CORC to their daily operations.

The first grouping of articles provides a "big picture" view of CORC. You
have already glanced, we hope, at **Jay Jordan**'s preface to this volume, which
demonstrates the OCLC CEO's high enthusiasm and commitment to the

[Haworth co-indexing entry note]: "Introduction." Calhoun, Karen, and John J. Riemer. Co-published
simultaneously in *Journal of Internet Cataloging* (The Haworth Information Press, an imprint of The
Haworth Press, Inc.) Vol. 4, No. 1/2, 2001, pp. 1-3; and: *CORC: New Tools and Possibilities for Cooperative
Electronic Resource Description* (ed: Karen Calhoun, and John J. Riemer) The Haworth Information Press,
an imprint of The Haworth Press, Inc., 2001, pp. 1-3. Single or multiple copies of this article are available for
a fee from The Haworth Document Delivery Service [1-800-342-9678, 9:00 a.m. - 5:00 p.m. (EST). E-mail
address: getinfo@haworthpressinc.com].

project. In his article, **Thomas Hickey**, OCLC Chief Scientist and CORC project director, provides a comprehensive treatment of the types of collaboration that form the basis for CORC's success so far, plans for more tightly integrating CORC with OCLC's WorldCat database, support for multiple metadata standards (Dublin Core, MARC), the challenges ahead for CORC, and much more. **Charlene Hurt and Bill Potter**'s paper offers two library directors' perspectives on how CORC might reshape library services and collections for the benefit of library users. **John Riemer**, in his piece on CORC and the Program for Cooperative Cataloging (PCC), discusses the potential synergism of these two international cooperatives and some ways their leaders and participants might correlate their actions and decisions.

The second group of articles offers a research and development view of CORC. **Lois Mai Chan and her co-authors** discuss the premise of Dublin Core (simplicity, semantic interoperability, flexibility); the complexity of Library of Congress Subject Headings (LCSH) and attempts at simplification; the conclusions of the ALCTS/SAC Subcommittee on Metadata and Subject Analysis; and research into faceted subject analysis in CORC using the FAST subject schema. **Carol Jean Godby and Ray Reighart** describe the WordSmith research project, whose goal is to obtain subject terminology directly from the text in Web documents. Their article covers the current implementation of WordSmith in CORC (i.e., the software and concepts behind what happens when a CORC user issues a command to "generate possible subject terms") and provides the results of an evaluation of WordSmith by CORC users. **Diane Vizine-Goetz**, a noted OCLC research scientist and renowned expert on classification, explores the potential of the Dewey Decimal Classification (DDC) system for helping CORC users assign classification numbers and subject headings. Her article offers insights into the use of the enhanced DDC database in CORC and explains how to interpret and employ LCSH/DDC mappings in CORC records. Her commentary on Scorpion-assigned DDC numbers (i.e., CORC's semi-automatic classification tool) promises to be particularly helpful to readers. **Eric Childress**, a key player in OCLC's development of CORC functions and features, discusses in detail the crosswalk that makes it possible for CORC users to view any record in the database as a MARC or Dublin Core record. Support for multiple metadata standards in a single system is one of the most striking characteristics of CORC.

The third and fourth groupings of articles represent implementers' views of CORC. In the third grouping, librarians report on implementations of CORC within cataloging and within cross-functional teams. **Jeff Edmunds and Roger Brisson**, cataloging and digital access specialists at Penn State, offer a "hands-on" glimpse of what it is like to catalog Internet resources in CORC. They comment on CORC's automatically generated metadata, classification, and subject terms; discuss the authority control features of CORC;

and offer suggestions for improvement of the system. **Norm Medeiros, Robert McDonald**, and **Paul Wrynn** analyze the appeal and value of CORC for library users, based on their utilization of CORC at the library of the New York University School of Medicine. They discuss how they decided what to select, what selectors need to know about CORC, and the experiences of using CORC and Dublin Core records as a basis for developing subject-specific Web pages (i.e., pathfinders) for biomedical resources. Readers who are interested in developing pathfinders as prominent research tools for library patrons are likely to find their article of interest. **Ann Caldwell, Dominique Coulombe, Ronald Fark**, and **Michael Jackson** at Brown University discuss how representatives from several functional groups used CORC to identify and select no-fee Web resources, develop pathfinders, gain electronic resource cataloging experience, and provide an opportunity for technical-public services staff collaboration. They found the CORC project promoted a new recognition of shared values among catalogers and reference librarians at Brown. **Karen Calhoun** describes the "CORC at Cornell" project, which was also undertaken by a cross-functional team. After describing the experimental workflow that was developed and tested in the project, she employs systems analysis techniques to model and discuss the potential of a widely distributed resource description process.

The fourth grouping of articles deals with using CORC and Dublin Core for special categories of materials. **Wayne Jones** of MIT assesses the adequacy of Dublin Core for describing serials. **Ann Hanlon and Ann Copeland** of the University of Illinois discuss using CORC's implementation of Dublin Core to create resource descriptions for the *@art gallery*, an online gallery of the university's school of art and design. **David Allen** of SUNY Stonybrook presents a set of insights and recommendations for the maps cataloging community. He deals with digital images of maps previously published on paper and offers interesting examples of Dublin Core cataloging of varying complexity.

Through their creative efforts today, this volume's authors are building the future of libraries. We offer them our respect and thanks. We also thank Ruth Carter (*JIC* editor) and The Haworth Press for the opportunity to gather and disseminate this volume on CORC. A blend of the theoretical and practical, the broad-based and specialized, the articles offer a variety of viewpoints. We believe that there is something here for any reader in the library and information science community who has an interest in online systems for Internet resource discovery, description and retrieval.

Collaboration in CORC

Thomas B. Hickey

SUMMARY. OCLC's Cooperative Online Resource Catalog (CORC) brings collaboration of the type long practiced by libraries to the description of Internet resources. Begun as a research project in 1998, it is now being developed into a full OCLC service. CORC users share a centralized database of resource descriptions accessed and edited through Web browsers. Collaboration within the project occurs on a number of levels to allow sharing of information within and among institutions around the world. By working closely with an enthusiastic group of interested libraries and librarians, we have concentrated on rapid interactive development while actually running a prototype service. Specific features that facilitate collaboration in CORC include Unicode support, strong support for the entry and linking of authority records, and support of multiple metadata formats. CORC is closely integrated with existing MARC21 systems, such as OCLC's WorldCat, while also supporting newer metadata formats, such as Dublin Core. This integration has proven to be both one of the most attractive features of CORC, as well as a continuing challenge. *[Article copies available for a fee from The Haworth Document Delivery Service: 1-800-342-9678. E-mail address: <getinfo@haworthpressinc.com> Website: <http://www.HaworthPress.com>]*

KEYWORDS. Collaboration, cooperation, CORC, digital libraries, Dublin Core, OCLC, pathfinders, RDF, XML

INTRODUCTION

Libraries have a long tradition of cooperation and collaboration. Library consortia in the United States can trace their roots back to at least to the 19th

Thomas B. Hickey is Chief Scientist, OCLC Office of Research, and Director of the CORC project.

[Haworth co-indexing entry note]: "Collaboration in CORC." Hickey, Thomas B. Co-published simultaneously in *Journal of Internet Cataloging* (The Haworth Information Press, an imprint of The Haworth Press, Inc.) Vol. 4, No. 1/2, 2001, pp. 5-16; and: *CORC: New Tools and Possibilities for Cooperative Electronic Resource Description* (ed: Karen Calhoun, and John J. Riemer) The Haworth Information Press, an imprint of The Haworth Press, Inc., 2001, pp. 5-16. Single or multiple copies of this article are available for a fee from The Haworth Document Delivery Service [1-800-342-9678, 9:00 a.m. - 5:00 p.m. (EST). E-mail address: getinfo@haworthpressinc.com].

5

century, and cooperative cataloging projects have been in place since the 1870s.[1] Until the growth of automation and telecommunication, cooperative cataloging was primarily done at a few major institutions (notably the Library of Congress) and distributed to others.[2] Online catalogs have allowed much wider participation in the creation of cataloging, which is fortunate, as it is not clear what the role of centralized cataloging will be for Web resources.

The OCLC Cooperative Online Resource Catalog (CORC) is a project designed to encourage and enhance the description of Web resources to better serve library patrons. The project started in OCLC's Office of Research in August 1998.[3] After several months of design and development, the first libraries started describing Web resources in January 1999. As of January 2000, there are about 200 libraries participating in the trial, and we are in the midst of turning the prototype system into a full OCLC service to be introduced later this year.

The concept behind CORC was developed in a series of meetings of OCLC's Office of Research. We gradually came to the conclusion that a system that concentrated on the collaborative development of a database of descriptions of Internet resources was something that was needed by libraries and something that OCLC should undertake. The size (and fluidity!) of the Web has already made cataloging a significant portion of it larger than any single organization could undertake by itself, and a shared system seemed the only alternative. OCLC had an earlier project, InterCat,[4] that developed standards and promoted our existing cataloging service for cataloging Internet resources, but a new system would make possible much easier experimentation and the addition of new features that seem essential for a system designed for the Web. Existing OCLC projects, such as Mantis,[5] a generalized XML editing tool, our work with the Dublin Core,[6] and other research gave us the tools and experience needed to create the system in a reasonable amount of time.

CORC has a number of distinguishing characteristics. The most striking one to many librarians is the support for multiple metadata standards within a single system. In fact, any bibliographic record within CORC can be viewed in a standard MARC21[7] view or as a Dublin Core record. Data is moved between the views by logic contained in tables and software procedures in a way transparent to system users. Other characteristics of CORC worth noting are the ability to create a provisional record based on data harvested from a resource, the possibility of storing data local to an institution in its catalog, and the availability of automatic assignment/suggestion of Dewey Decimal Classification[8] numbers. I believe, however, that it is the emphasis on cooperation that differentiates CORC, if not from OCLC's current systems, then at least from the many other efforts to bring control over the raw Internet we are forced to cope with. A challenge for CORC is to take what has been cooperation in the past and enhance it to reach something more like collaboration for the future.

CORC represents the largest effort so far to apply library techniques to describing the Web. Many other projects are attempting to provide better access to the Web (for example, in the IMesh[9] community of subject gateways or the Librarians' Index to the Internet),[10] but without the same level of collaboration and integration with current library systems.

LEVELS AND TYPES OF COOPERATION

Cataloging cooperation can be broadly divided into four areas:

- Labor; Who will do what
- Standards; How they will do it
- Systems; What they will use to do it
- Delivery; How the metadata is used

CORC is primarily involved in the systems and standards areas, with some emphasis on delivery. Many of the levels and types of cooperation in CORC will be no surprise to librarians or catalogers; they have been cooperating in these ways for many years. Others are more unique to CORC and its technology. In combination, these varieties of cooperation reinforce each other and become extremely powerful.

Division of labor, trying to divide libraries for coverage of certain types of materials or subjects, has never been a priority at OCLC, and CORC is no exception. We make few recommendations on what to catalog beyond considering local resources first. In the future we may be able to identify system features that would help libraries and library consortia to manage this process better, but so far this is an area not addressed by CORC.

Standards are the mainstay of library cooperation. Without some standards, one library's contribution to a database will not be of much use to another library. Much of this work, such as the Dublin Core standardization effort, goes on outside of the CORC project itself, but within CORC certain standards and procedures governing the application of international standards have to be done. The Dublin Core, for example, allows all fields to be optional, while within the library community some slightly more prescriptive levels need to be established.

We call the main bibliographic database within CORC the Resource Catalog. This catalog itself is an important part of enabling cooperation. It is through the Resource Catalog that libraries can see and use records that others have created, as well as share the maintenance of those records. Auxiliary to the Resource Catalog, in the production system, there will be a savefile. CORC's savefile design expands on the savefile idea pioneered by OCLC's Cataloging service, giving expanded options to track and manage records within an institution.

Records within the Resource Catalog, of course, are where the most visible activity occurs. This is becoming more complicated as we prepare CORC for production. CORC participants have persuaded us to support a strong relationship between WorldCat and CORC. This has led us to decide that a version of each CORC record will reside in OCLC's WorldCat database in addition to the CORC catalog. This will make them available within the existing OCLC Cataloging service, greatly strengthening the usefulness of CORC.

CORC has also developed the idea of electronic *pathfinders*. Beyond access to the database via Z39.50 and FirstSearch, these are our main approach to the problem of delivering metadata to end-users. Pathfinders in CORC appear to end-users as collections of links with associated descriptions, essentially online bibliographies. As built within the system, these may include direct links into the Resource Catalog, searches of it, and other hand-created links to resources. Links that are made through the Catalog, however, allow the sharing of the maintenance of URL links, since the records displayed to users are extracted from the shared catalog and benefit from updates to the catalog, rather than being from a static page of descriptions and links.

Finally, the whole process used in developing CORC has been a model of how a system can be designed by library practitioners in coordination with a not-for-profit corporation.

CORC'S IMPLEMENTATION

The CORC system enables cooperation at several levels:

- Within institutions
  - Enhanced workflow tracking
  - Movement between collection development, reference and technical processing
- Across institutions
  - Shared creation/maintenance in the Resource Catalog
  - Member input authorities
- Around the World
  - International standards
  - Multiple scripts
- Across systems
  - Interactions with WorldCat
  - Interactions with NACO (Name Authority Cooperative Program)

The Resource Catalog is the primary vehicle for collaboration. Within the catalog, collaboration occurs immediately on the attempted creation of a record via an automatic search for matching URLs. Finding an already created record that can be reused is one the largest benefits of working in a shared cataloging system. Currently within CORC, users are informed of the existence of not just completed records, but also of the URL and title of records that have not yet been released for general use.

If someone is actually in the process of editing a resource, the record is locked, preventing conflicting edits happening simultaneously to a record. This will become more complicated in the future as we become much more tightly integrated with OCLC's WorldCat. WorldCat is a large (more than 40 million records) database maintained by over 7,000 libraries, and the CORC database, to be viable, needs to interact well with it. Our plan is to have 'mirror' records in WorldCat for each CORC record. This design will allow editing of records on either system. CORC will be able to lock WorldCat records so that changes made to records in CORC that affect the 'master' record can be immediately reflected in WorldCat. Since WorldCat will not be able to lock and replace CORC records in real-time, changes made to World-Cat from OCLC Cataloging service will be merged into CORC on a nightly basis. This greatly expands the usefulness of the CORC database by making it available to all WorldCat users, not only librarians, but also library patrons that access it through FirstSearch.

Accomplishing this integration does raise a number of difficult policy and systems problems that need to be solved to make the whole system work in a reasonable way. In general, the WorldCat record will function as the 'master' record; however, there are many exceptions. There are a number of differences between the two catalogs in the imposition of field length limitations, character sets, and treatment of institution specific data. The CORC record will have information specific to metadata formats not supported by World-Cat, which have to be maintained in concert with MARC information. From a systems viewpoint, these problems are similar to (and involved with) those encountered in converting between Dublin Core and MARC. Treatment of these differences across the catalogs needs to be as sophisticated as possible to produce the 'right' result while still maintaining a relatively usable user interface.

Fairly intense collaboration on the creation of bibliographic records often occurs within a given institution as several people become involved in the creation and editing of records. CORC is adapting and extending ideas from the Cataloging service and CORC into a Savefile that will offer full biblio-graphic searching as well as sorting by library-assigned status fields. This should help track individual records as well as collections of records (more about collections below). It appears that the support of Dublin Core within

CORC also contributes to intra-institutional cooperation by making it possible and attractive for non-catalogers to participate in the selection and initial description of resources. The Dublin Core's English-language headings and simplified view of the data make it much more attractive and accessible to non-catalogers. Along these same lines, there is an OCLC research project looking at simplifying Library of Congress Subject Headings[11] by breaking them into facets, which should make the application of LCSH available to non-specialists. The possibility of local data stored in the records, that is only displayed within a given institution, also greatly expands the capabilities of the system.

AUTHORITY CONTROL

Authority control is another area where libraries, especially in the English-speaking world, have developed a remarkable process for creating and using controlled forms of headings. We feel that establishing authority links within the metadata for electronic resources is one of the key capabilities that libraries can offer in "controlling" the Internet. To make it easier to do this, we are adding the capability of creating "member input" authority records. These records may or may not become national authority records through the existing NACO[12] process. Adding the ability for 'ordinary' librarians to create authorities should help the whole authority control process. In many cases the local librarian may have personal information about the creator of a resource that would be very difficult to capture in any other way. By making it possible for these member input authority records to eventually feed into NACO, we are leveraging the NACO process and expanding the ability for non-NACO libraries to contribute their knowledge and expertise.

New standards are also opening up the possibility of greater international cooperation in authority control. For example, Die Deutsche Bibliothek is spearheading an effort to create a Dublin Core authorities standard that could greatly facilitate the exchange and linking of authorities across existing systems. We eventually plan to implement what is often called "access control"[13] within CORC, so that a German speaker could search and display records with the German form of a name if it is available, while a Chinese speaker would see a different form. These efforts are worthy of their own paper as we get further along with them, and I won't be discussing them further here.

STANDARDS

Standards make it possible to reuse others' metadata. As any library system must, we deal with standards for access, resource description, and interchange, in addition to honoring the standards for harvesters and robots on the Web.

New metadata standards are appearing at a dizzying pace. Most of this development is happening outside of CORC proper, but we are consulting with the Library of Congress in the development of their crosswalk showing the relationship between elements of the Dublin Core and MARC fields,[14] and we plan to implement that crosswalk. OCLC is a leader in the Dublin Core effort, and CORC team members participate in both MARC and Dublin Core standards development. Supporting multiple standards within the same framework is difficult and is an ongoing process as we refine our mappings and algorithms. It seems essential, though, if we are to integrate existing library systems with new standards and approaches to metadata. Internally, we are in the process of converting the Resource Catalog into Unicode. This will, of course, offer some interesting challenges when exporting records in the MARC format, but we expect that the increase in functionality, especially for non-roman scripts, will be tremendous.

Supporting multiple metadata standards and, especially, offering RDF/XML[15] opens the possibility of interacting with other communities. It appears as though the whole world is just discovering metadata, and it is apparent that the better libraries can exchange metadata with others, whether they are museums, archives, publishers, manufacturers, authors or even librarians that have been using different systems, the better off we will be. While MARC21, especially for libraries in English speaking countries, has proved a durable tool for metadata creation and exchange, its acceptance in other countries has been slower, and it will probably never be used extensively outside of libraries. The continued development of the Dublin Core and metadata exchange standards, such as RDF, offers the first real possibility of easy worldwide exchange of cataloging.

COLLECTIONS

Libraries often generate or receive large batches of metadata from various sources that need to be tracked and manipulated as a group, and this is becoming even more common as more librarians work with electronic resources that can be searched and selected en masse. In many cases, these groups of records are, indeed, a collection that needs to maintain its identity beyond initial processing. CORC will support collections within the Resource Catalog through the planned ability to name and manipulate groups of records within the Savefile and full indexing of the Catalog, allowing retrieval. To present collections to library users, CORC's pathfinders offer the ability to collect and present groups of records, and by allowing pathfinders to point at other pathfinders to extend this to large sets of records.

Beyond these things, we see better support for collections as a challenge ahead of us. We need to understand the types of collections and operations needed for them, so that we can support the collaboration needed to both create and maintain collections across institutional boundaries.

URL CHECKING

From a bibliographic control point of view, one of the nicest things about resources on the Web is that they all (almost by definition) have URLs associated with them. URLs give good identifiers to search on, but experience shows they are not infallible. Some of the problems we see are URLs in records that point to an associated resource, not the one being described, variations of the form of URLs to the same resource, and the well known problem of Web resources either moving their location, or disappearing altogether.

One of the simplest things we do with URLs is to check them against the current CORC file to see whether the resource has already been described. Even this match takes some ingenuity, as we find that a number of variations on the URL need to be searched for to start to get a comprehensive search (adding www., substituting htm for html, etc.). Actually, just storing the URL used to retrieve a resource for description turns out not to be enough. A large number of URLs get redirected before a Web user actually gets to the resource itself, and any of these intermediate URLs are also potential identifiers for the resource, so we capture those when possible and match against them when retrieving on URL. Occasionally, a URL in a metadata record is not the URL of the resource itself, but refers to some other entity, such as the publisher. This is often questionable cataloging practice, but something that has to be taken into consideration in our system design, especially when attempting to automatically remove duplicates from the catalog.

Beyond the verification of the existence of a URL lies the checking of the content of the resource to see whether it has changed sufficiently to warrant a change in the associated metadata stored in CORC. Since some sites are continually changing (e.g., a newspaper site), just the fact that the page has changed is not necessarily an indication that the associated metadata must change. We have created research prototypes for detecting this, and OCLC currently runs similar scans for our NetFirst records, but we have not yet implemented them within CORC.

PATHFINDERS

Within libraries, the building of bibliographies often falls more into the reference services area rather than technical services. CORC has been developing the concept of pathfinders, borrowing the term from the paper path-finders often developed at libraries to guide patrons in the use of library resources within a certain topic. Pathfinders can tie the development of these bibliographies to the Resource Catalog and make them much easier to construct and maintain. So far, however, we have run into a number of problems trying to make pathfinders fit into the current library environment. This may be partially because reference librarians do not have as strong a tradition of sharing as catalogers have been forced to develop, but there are technical problems in making pages that may change quickly to be easily accessible within a library's Web pages.

The alternative is not very attractive, however. Libraries all over the world are creating and maintaining very similar pages, pointing to many of the same Web resources. As the resources change and move, the pages pointing to them become out of date and require a huge amount of duplicative work to maintain. Surely, there is a model of cooperation that will be more sensible. This is an area where we may need to somehow develop a 'critical mass' of pages in CORC before the system becomes generally useful.

THE CORC DEVELOPMENT PROCESS

In many ways the actual development process of CORC has been a study in collaboration. We started recruiting libraries almost immediately after the project was conceived, and were very lucky in having enthusiastic coopera-tion of the libraries of the CIC (Committee on Institutional Cooperation; the academic consortium of the Big Ten universities and the University of Chica-go). The University of Michigan Library was particularly helpful. There is nothing like having real users with real problems when developing a system!

CORC-L is an active e-mail discussion list letting CORC users communi-cate among themselves with OCLC participation. In fact, the whole develop-ment team subscribes to CORC-L, so there is a good chance that notes are at least read by the people directly involved in implementation. We also have a CORC-system e-mail address for more specific questions to the CORC team, and that is monitored not only by those working directly on CORC, but by a number of people all over OCLC who want to keep informed on what users are experiencing.

OCLC has always tried to stay in contact with its users, but the Internet now makes this practical in a much more meaningful way. E-mail is not a substitute for face-to-face interaction, but is about the only way for a geo-graphically dispersed group to interact closely on design. Although electron-ic, it has offered the first example I have seen of day-to-day personal interac-tion between users of our systems and the developers actually writing the code for them. Users with a problem will frequently be corresponding direct-ly with the programmers that are responsible for the involved code.

To collaborate in person, OCLC has sponsored two on-site meetings of participants that have been very well attended (about 90 participants at each), as well as meetings at American Library Association annual and mid-winter conventions. The on-site meetings are most important from a development point of view, since there is time to explain what we are doing, listen to what the users are doing (or trying to do), and actually collect priorities based on their needs and desires. In addition, all of the CORC developers can attend, not just the limited number that attend the conventions. One of our more popular activities at these meetings is to have a whole series of sessions where various developers sit down with volunteers who can show them how they use CORC and explain what they like and where they see problems.

There is no doubt that the level of interaction and interest of the CORC users has made the project extremely satisfying both professionally and per-sonally for many of the CORC team members and probably also for many CORC users.

MAJOR CHALLENGES

The main challenge CORC faces is not that different than the challenge libraries face: we must accommodate the changes we see in the metadata and library worlds while maintaining reasonable compatibility with our legacy systems. The changes we see driving this are the proliferation in metadata standards, the inclusion of non-catalogers (and even non-librarians) in meta-data creation, the changing nature of the resources that need description, and the possibility for much greater interaction and cooperation at all levels. Our approach is to develop CORC as rapidly as we can, extend and expand rather than replace, and do our utmost to listen and respond to both current and potential creators and maintainers of metadata.

Associated with this challenge is understanding how relevant our current models are when dealing with the Web. A good example of this is the impor-tance in the United States, and increasingly around the world, of the catalog-ing done at the Library of Congress. In the current library world, this catalog-ing forms the mainstay of OCLC's WorldCat and any other catalog of such material. The existence of this file was undoubtedly instrumental in the early success of OCLC. Is there the equivalent for the Web, and if not, should there be? We 'seeded' the CORC database with about 200,000 records derived from WorldCat and OCLC's NetFirst database of Internet resources. Will there continue to be a 'core' set of records that should be created by a central organization, or can this now be done in a much more distributed manner?

Another example of the possible clash between existing ideas and the Web is how far the model of 'holdings' works with the Web. In the physical world it has been fairly clear what it means that a library holds a book or journal. Is simply being interested in a Web resource the equivalent? How interested are libraries in descriptions of free sites on the Internet? Interested enough to want to get new versions of such records as others modify them? What will be the level of reuse of metadata records? This is of great importance in any analysis of the economic benefit of shared databases. Is it in local catalogs that these records will be the most used, or via remote access, or a more complex model?

Even though collaboration and cooperation are at the heart of CORC, there is still more to do to promote cooperation. Our current systems provide little or no feedback to creators of records of how they are modified and used. It is also difficult to know what sort of records others are working on and to ask questions of others. One can imagine a system that promotes collaboration by providing help in managing resource selection across a variety of libraries, including rankings based on usage. Systems could also raise the level of collaboration by inviting and managing comments from catalog users.

CORC continues and expands a long tradition of library cooperation. It supports a transformation in the nature of library cataloging and in the catalog itself, and represents an unparalleled initiative to allow librarians to leverage what they know about organizing information and apply it to the Web. OCLC and its library partners have met many challenges in bringing CORC to its current level of development; many more challenges remain. In particular, we face many policy and systems problems associated with turning the CORC prototype into a production system. We are confident, however, that through continued collaboration, these challenges will be overcome.

NOTES

1. Kopp, James J. Library Consortia and Information Technology: The Past, the Present, the Promise. *Information Technology and Libraries*. March 1998, pp. 7-12.

2. Tillett, Barbara B. Catalog It Once for All: A History of Cooperative Cataloging in the United States Prior to 1967 (Before MARC). *Cataloging & Classification Quarterly*. 17 No. 3/4, 1993, pp. 3-38.

3. Hickey, Thomas B., Childress, Eric, and Watson, Bradley. The genesis and development of CORC as an OCLC Office of Research project. *OCLC Newsletter*. No. 239, May/June 1999. Available at: *http://www.oclc.org/oclc/new/n239/feature/02feature. htm.*

4. OCLC Office of Research. InterCat Project. Available at: *http://www.oclc. org/oclc/research/projects/intercat.htm.*

5. Shafer, Keith. Mantis Home Page. *http://purl.oclc.org/mantis/.*

6. Dublin Core Metadata Initiative. Available at: *http://purl.org/DC.*

7. MARC Standards MARC21. Library of Congress Network Development and MARC Standards Office. Available at: *http://lcweb.loc.gov/marc/index.html.*

8. OCLC Forest Press. Dewey Decimal System Home Page. *http://www.oclc.org/oclc/fp/index.htm.*

9. International Collaboration on Internet Subject Gateways. Available at: *http://www.imesh.org/.* See also *http://www.desire.org/html/subjectgateways/community/imesh.*

10. Librarians Index to the Internet. Available at: *http://lii.org/.*

11. Library of Congress, Cataloging Distribution Service. Tools for Authority Control–Subject Headings. *http://lcweb.loc.gov/cds/lcsh.html.*

12. NACO Program for Cooperative Cataloging. Available at: *http://lcweb.loc.gov/catdir/pcc/naco.html.*

13. Tillett, Barbara. International Shared Resource Records for Controlled Access. Available at: *http://www.oclc.org/oclc/man/authconf/tillett.htm.* In: Authority Control in the 21st Century: An Invitational Conference, March 1996. Available at: *http://www.oclc.org/oclc/man/authconf/procmain.htm.*

14. Dublin Core/MARC/GILS Crosswalk. *http://lcweb.loc.gov/marc/dccross.html.*

15. W3C. Resource Description Framework (RDF). Available at: *http://www.w3.org/RDF/.*

CORC and the Future of Libraries: Two University Librarians' Perspectives

Charlene Hurt
William Gray Potter

SUMMARY. Two University Librarians look at OCLC's CORC project from the perspective of how it helps achieve the goals of the evolution of the virtual library as well as their individual library goal of creating an all-inclusive catalog of the information provided to library users. They also examine the implications of the CORC process on library organizations, including the potential to involve a much wider range of participants in a CORC project. *[Article copies available for a fee from The Haworth Document Delivery Service: 1-800-342-9678. E-mail address: <getinfo@haworthpressinc.com> Website: <http://www.HaworthPress.com>]*

KEYWORDS. CORC, OCLC, virtual library, Dublin Core, cataloging, Internet, Web, library administrators, library organization

The Cooperative Online Resource Catalog (CORC) project of OCLC offers library administrators an opportunity to realize a goal which has long eluded them–an all-inclusive catalog of resources the library offers. The avenue to realizing this goal is both high tech and traditional–a technology-based tool to simplify the process of cataloging records and a process based

Charlene Hurt is University Librarian at Georgia State University (e-mail: libcsh@langate.gsu.edu) and William Gray Potter is University Librarian at the University of Georgia (e-mail: wpotter@arches.uga.edu).

[Haworth co-indexing entry note]: "CORC and the Future of Libraries: Two University Librarians' Perspectives." Hurt, Charlene, and William Gray Potter. Co-published simultaneously in *Journal of Internet Cataloging* (The Haworth Information Press, an imprint of The Haworth Press, Inc.) Vol. 4, No. 1/2, 2001, pp. 17-27; and: *CORC: New Tools and Possibilities for Cooperative Electronic Resource Description* (ed: Karen Calhoun, and John J. Riemer) The Haworth Information Press, an imprint of The Haworth Press, Inc., 2001, pp. 17-27. Single or multiple copies of this article are available for a fee from The Haworth Document Delivery Service [1-800-342-9678, 9:00 a.m. - 5:00 p.m. (EST). E-mail address: getinfo@haworthpressinc.com].

on collective effort by the library community. CORC provides the tools that simplify and integrate the cataloging of a wide range of library resources that have been difficult to organize and control. These tools are described elsewhere in considerable detail.[1] As library administrators our interest is in how CORC can help us reshape our services and collections to meet the challenges of libraries in the digital age. Two areas we'd like to discuss are how CORC can influence the evolution of the virtual library and how CORC can be a vehicle for organizational development and change.

CORC AND THE VIRTUAL LIBRARY

The digital library is not merely equivalent to a digitized collection with information management tools. It is rather an environment to bring together collections, services, and people in support of the full life cycle of creation, dissemination, use, and preservation of data, information, and knowledge.[2]

From this quote, it can be seen that the virtual library is very much like the physical library. All the things that happen in a physical library should also be supported in the virtual library. We might think of it as a new branch library–or perhaps as a new main library.

For most libraries today, our virtual library is our presence on the Web–our home page or our Web site. For better or worse, this is how we are offering our virtual libraries. We use established authoring tools to create Web sites. Some libraries have prepared very sophisticated Web sites, others have simply listed library services and electronic resources. One thing is certain–every library is doing it their own way.

Library sites are among the best Web sites available. They are usually free. Even when they link to commercial products that are restricted to that library's home community, they still do a better job of organizing a wide range of resources than most commercial or other sites. They also serve to filter out the noise. Librarians across the country have used their training and their commitment to public service to select resources on the Web and then create Web sites that provide an organized and coherent approach to those resources.

Libraries select and organize what is free on the Internet. We also purchase, either individually or together through consortia, what is worth purchasing for our communities. Consortial Web sites bring together what we acquire as groups, while individual library sites are more tailored to local needs.

As you look at library Web sites today, you begin to see some common components of the emerging virtual library. These components include:

- online catalogs, especially of the local library
- abstracting and indexing databases
- full text/images of periodicals
- e-journals
- reference works
- full text literary databases
- recommended Internet resources
- electronic pathfinders
- electronic reserves
- digitized collections
- finding aids for special collections
- local information on collections and services
- local information on departments, people, etc.
- link to a consortium Web site
- links to community information

While these are emerging as common elements, the fact is that each library has its own site, and each site is very different. Even though each offers similar products and services, the organization of each is very different. Consortial Web sites are usually more focused and better organized, but even here each consortial site is different.

One of the virtues of libraries, as they have evolved over the past several centuries, is that each is organized around a set of commonly accepted practices and standards. If you learn to use one, you can usually find your way around any other one. Libraries are predictable. They offer a catalog, a reference desk, a circulation desk, books shelved according to a standard classification, and dedicated, helpful librarians. As you move from one library to another, what you have learned from other libraries helps you understand a new library. There will always be some idiosyncrasies, but for the most part we follow practices that have evolved, that have been tested by experience. Once you have learned how one works, you can move fairly easily to other libraries and to larger libraries.

With physical libraries, we have a unifying metaphor, a model that has served us well. With the virtual library, we have a profusion of library Web sites with no unifying metaphor, no accepted model, little commonality in what we offer, and no consistency of organization. The result is that readers are confused as they move within a library site and as they move from one library site to another. It is as if there is a belief that Web site design should address particular local needs. This would be analogous to using catalog rules and subject headings that fit local needs. Of course, this was the case up through most of the 19th century. Over the past 100 years, we learned to agree to standards based upon experience. The time has come to do the same thing with the design of library Web sites and the design of the virtual libraries we are offering.

Librarians have long seen the need for standards because they serve the needs of the reader. We, of course, all believe that the needs of the reader come first. As we have done before, we need to cooperatively determine the best principles of design and organization and agree to abide by them. This is an evolving process, but we need to recognize that we are in the middle of the process. We have encouraged 1,000 flowers to bloom. Now we need to weed and cultivate.

How can we do this? We can look at how our predecessors did it and work through our professional organizations to recognize and define the best practices for Web site design. We can also look to the past to see how we achieved great things and try to learn from those efforts.

One of our greatest achievements, because it shows what can be done when we work together for a common goal, is the original OCLC. WorldCat (the former Online Union Catalog) is the closest we have ever come to the 19th century vision of a universal bibliography, a single source that catalogs every book ever published.

The twin to the dream of the universal bibliography was the all inclusive catalog, a library catalog that reflected everything that a given library offered. The catalog should include not just books, but also journal articles, the contents of the vertical file, manuscript collections, and everything else contained in a library collection. It was this ideal that led H.W. Wilson to initially offer the Readers' Guide to Periodical Literature cards that could be filed directly into a library's catalog. Unfortunately, while we have realized the universal bibliography, we have drifted further away from the inclusive catalog. It proved to be too expensive to maintain with the card catalog and, as we have developed the online catalog, we have been overwhelmed with a profusion of new resources that should be entered into a truly inclusive catalog. The wealth of new physical resources–film, records, video tapes, manuscript collections, etc.–was daunting enough, but now we have all the electronic resources that should also be included.

There is hope, though. Just as OCLC delivered the universal bibliography, they now offer a tool that can provide the inclusive catalog. CORC's immediate purpose is actually to expand the universal bibliography to include all the things that will not fit or that are difficult to fit into WorldCat, such as long records or specialized formats like the MARC cataloging for manuscript collections. However, CORC's next purpose is to provide every library with a way of cataloging all the resources that we did not have the time or the means to catalog before. Further, CORC provides us with the means to integrate all those records into one catalog.

It is important to recognize that CORC operates on two levels–the universal bibliography and the inclusive catalog. One level is global and one level is local. The two are, of course, intertwined and sometimes difficult to separate. With WorldCat, the distinction was easy to see. Global records were in WorldCat, local records were downloaded into the local online catalog. With CORC, global records will exist in the larger, global file, but local records may reside there as well. A library may use CORC to catalog a local resource in the global file and then download it to a local database, as we do with online catalogs. Alternatively, a library may choose to have that local resource appear only in the global file and not maintain a local file.

For example, Georgia State University might use CORC to catalog a map from its special collections. A link would be established to an image of the map. The CORC record could reside in the global file and/or the local file in a SiteSearch database on GALILEO. The image of the map could also be located in both places. The location of the record and of the image may well become irrelevant because CORC provides the tools not only to create the record but also to search the local files and the global files seamlessly and return the desired results. Thus, if a library has cataloged all its maps on CORC, it can provide access to them through a search of a local catalog or through a search of the global CORC database restricted to that library's holdings. How it is done will be seamless to the reader.

Looking at the previously mentioned list of resources offered through library Web sites, CORC can be used to organize and catalog each of them. In most cases, the CORC can provide access on two levels. The first level is to catalog the resource as a bibliographic entity. The second level is to actually execute a search through a Z39.50 interface (see Table 1).[3]

CORC then gives us the capability to both catalog a resource and also to link to it for the purpose of executing a Z39.50 search of its specific contents. Of course, links would also be provided to any digitized documents, including full text, images, video, audio, etc.

What will the virtual library look like with CORC used to its full potential? The exact configuration needs to be refined and agreed to by the community. On the most important level, though, the virtual library becomes an inclusive catalog of all resources, print and electronic, local and remote, that a library selects to offer to its community. At an early stage of development, this would simply mean that a library would collect or build CORC records for everything it wants to include. In other words, we would catalog each resource as a bibliographic entity, as shown in the table. This collection of records could be mounted on a local file or tagged in the global CORC database. A reader searching this collection would be presented with a set of descriptive catalog or metadata records describing all the resources that might be of interest.

At a later stage of development, a reader would be presented with an

TABLE 1. How Various Resources Might Be Organized

Resource	Catalog as Entity	Z39.50 Interface
Online catalogs	Yes	Yes
Abstracting and indexing databases	Yes	Yes
Full text/images of periodicals	Yes	Yes, through A&I
E-journals	Yes	Yes, through A&I
Online reference works	Yes	Yes
Full text literary databases	Yes	Yes
Recommended Internet resources	Yes	Yes
Electronic pathfinders	Yes	Yes
Electronic reserves	Yes	Yes
Digitized collections	Yes	Yes
Finding aids for special collections	Yes	Yes
Local information on collections and services	Yes	Maybe
Local information on departments, people, etc.	Yes	Maybe
Link to a consortium Web site	Yes	Yes
Links to community information	Yes	Maybe

interface that would, in effect, formulate a search of all available resources. At this stage, we would use the Z39.50 interfaces as suggested in the table above. For example, if a reader at the University of Georgia were interested in looking for information on the Cherokee, the interface would formulate a search that would return a set of relevant resources. These resources would include books, manuscript collections, maps, journal articles, films, encyclopedia articles, and anything else that the library has chosen to include.

To summarize, libraries have always had collections that were not well controlled, e.g., special collections, manuscripts, archives, media, etc. These collections have proliferated with all the Web resources we now acquire. CORC gives us a means to unify these resources by offering a tool that generates records that fit MARC or Dublin Core. Using CORC, we can catalog Web sites, e-journals, and other new e-resources. It can also be used to control collections we have not been able to include. The ideal has always been to build an inclusive catalog, to include everything in a collection. CORC gives us the means to realize that ideal and go beyond by including not just what is owned but what we simply provide access to as well. CORC can be the means to establish a uniform and predictable virtual library that meets the needs of all readers.

CORC AND LIBRARY ORGANIZATION

As discussed above, OCLC's CORC project offers substantial benefits to libraries and to OCLC, and motivation to participate is intrinsic to the nature of the project and the high value librarians place on cooperative endeavors. There is, however, an additional motivation for a library administrator to pledge library resources towards participation in the project. For library managers who are seeking to evolve their libraries and library staffs into organizations better able to adapt to the new millennium, CORC offers an unprecedented opportunity to reconsider working relationships within the context of a new intellectual framework.

This organizational impact derives from the nature of the content that CORC seeks to catalog, and from the methodology of the project. Since the content is the World Wide Web, including pathfinders mounted there by individual libraries, CORC covers an area more likely to be viewed as in the realm of librarians outside of the catalog department. There are a variety of titles for librarians who spend considerable time identifying and creating Web sites, such as bibliographers, information consultants, or reference, liaison, or collection development librarians. On Georgia State University's campus, the liaison librarians (who are also reference and collection development librarians) are actively identifying and creating Web sites, particularly in their subject areas, and are developing individual Web sites on various topics that incorporate reputable Web sites. Another important group of librarians deeply involved in the Web are library faculty in special collections and archives, many of who are creating digital archives to add to the content of the Web's virtual library.

The methodology of the CORC project is the second factor to consider in deciding where the work on the project can be done. As mentioned above, the other value of CORC is that it provides a tool set to create and maintain these records in files apart from the traditional catalog files, files that are and should be the purview of professional catalogers. This allows the distribution of CORC cataloging responsibility to departments in the library that have not previously cataloged their resources. Once a Web site or local resource is identified as worthy of inclusion in the catalog of the virtual library, CORC provides a tool which automatically harvests the information from the Web site and creates a basic Dublin Core record. This Dublin Core record may need to be corrected or enhanced, but it does not require the complex processes involved with creating a MARC record. Librarians can create a new CORC record without "speaking MARC." The Dublin Core record is designed, however, to map to MARC if that additional step is desired, although intervention of a MARC-speaker would probably be needed. Some participants in the CORC project are converting all the records to MARC, while others are stopping at the creation of the Dublin Core record and others are doing some of both. Any cataloging record created via CORC can be exported as metadata for embedding within any e-resource the library has control over and which is not already endowed with the metadata. At this time the project allows any of those choices.

Some catalogers may be uncomfortable with this seeming intrusion into their territory, but they need not be. The fact is that a major portion of every library's collection has gone uncataloged in the past because we did not have enough staff to fully catalog everything, and we did not have tools to provide an appropriate lesser level of cataloging. As a result, special collections, media, and reference departments tended to create finding aids and small databases of their own to track this material. CORC provides a means to replace these specialized, often homegrown, approaches that is easy to use and can be integrated into a search of the main catalog without compromising its integrity.

We need to recognize that there are no villains here. Catalogers are not the problem. They have not been able to keep up with the growing profusion of resources that have flooded libraries. The central responsibility of the catalog department has been and must remain the bibliographic control of the traditional library collection, while extending the catalog to new resources as appropriate. Beyond that, catalog departments need to be involved in establishing guidelines and procedures for using CORC and similar tools to expand bibliographic control to the whole collection.

The degree to which a CORC record is integrated into the library's own catalog and decisions about how CORC should be integrated in OCLC's WorldCat will require the intellectual efforts of catalogers, who need to be involved in establishing guidelines and procedures for using CORC to expand bibliographic control to the whole collection. The cataloger's expertise is vital to this process. The cataloger's labor is not. Instead, that labor can be decentralized to the departments that actually house and use the resources. CORC provides the means to make this possible.

Academic libraries throughout the country are involved in changing their organizations to adapt to the new realities of university libraries today, including but not limited to the enormous technological advances we see everyday. Librarians are also concerned with threat to freedom of access to information for scholarly work, and with the profusion of biased and unreliable information readily available to our students. Academic librarians are involved in a number of initiatives related to these concerns, including CORC and the Scholarly Publishing and Academic Resources Coalition (SPARC) project for alternative scholarly publishing. A recent initiative emerged at a meeting of library leaders jointly sponsored by ARL and OCLC in September 1999 at Keystone, Colorado. The group drafted the "Keystone Principles," which form the basis upon which additional action plans are being developed. The principles were also endorsed by the fall meeting of the Association of Southeastern Research Libraries and the winter board meeting of the Association of College and Research Libraries.[4] Inherent in those principles is the commitment to re-engineer libraries to meet the challenges academic libraries face, even if that means giving up some of the things we traditionally do. The Keystone Principles talk about the importance of the library reasserting its role as the heart of the university or, in more modern parlance, its intellectual commons. One way to achieve this is for the library to become the "portal of choice" for members of the academic community when they are seeking scholarly and reliable information. Another principle emphasizes the importance of libraries being creators and assemblers of databases. There is a strong commitment to integrating libraries more closely into the academic programs of the university and to assuring that all students become "information literate" during their college years. Applying the Keystone Principles to decisions about how libraries should allocate their resources provides a framework for making difficult decisions and is well-suited to a discussion about whether a library should undertake participation in the CORC project.

Although participation in the CORC project doesn't require identification of a particular group of records or specific topic areas, some of the participants had, so to speak, laid claim to certain areas of the Web universe. The GALILEO CORC Representative at the University of Georgia, for example, had determined that he would concentrate first on Georgia resources, especially those in GALILEO. At least one group of specialized librarians among the CORC project participants has decided to work together to cover Web sites and pathfinders in their area of expertise.[5]

The CORC project had also been talking about identifying and cataloging pathfinders in various subject areas, as a logical extension of cataloging the Web. In a related development, a subcommittee of the Keystone group is working on a proposal to develop a Web site for core pathfinders, giving further impetus to the interest in this topic. The concept of developing a standard format for a group of pathfinders that can be used as templates by individual librarians has much to recommend it.

Putting together the call to action of the Keystone Principles and the opportunity to participate in the CORC project was primarily a matter of serendipity at Georgia State University, but each reinforced the other. For Pullen Library, the two initiatives responded directly to the goals of our own strategic plan, which called for greater involvement in the teaching and learning process, leadership in the use of information technology, and participation in the wider community of library professionals concerned with equity of access to information. Our challenge was to find a way to have participation in the CORC project help us achieve our goals.

We had initially assumed that CORC would be a task for the Catalog

Department–not an easy task in a year when MARCIVE authority control and government documents records were scheduled to be loaded into a new online catalog and all the University System libraries in Georgia are engaged in developing a new union catalog. As we learned more about CORC, we realized how well it lends itself to cross-departmental work, since public service librarians can identify the significant Web sites, harvest them for basic Dublin Core records, edit the Dublin Core records to the degree required, and pass them along to the Catalog Department for further development into MARC records. Since CORC records won't be integrated into the online catalog, at least for now, issues of responsibility for the integrity of the database can be avoided, and not all CORC records would have to be developed into MARC records, thereby avoiding some of the problems related to the limited time available from Catalogers.

Pullen Library has particular strength in the area of music, including a music liaison librarian who is active in publishing, several librarians who are particularly knowledgeable about music, and a special collections and archives department which holds the Johnny Mercer archives and has two archivists with considerable expertise in music. We also have a liaison from the Music Department who is actively engaged in building our collection. This suggested that music might be a good area on which to focus. What we proposed is that our CORC project be a collaborative effort between the liaison librarians, Special Collections and Archives, the Catalog Department, and faculty and graduate assistants from the School of Music. This approach provides us with a way to realize many of our goals: greater integration into the academic programs of the university, participation in creating and assembling databases, commitment to information literacy training for our students, and technological innovation. It also forces us to break down walls between the various departments of the library and create new working relationships. CORC projects would lend themselves particularly well to a team-based environment, which many libraries, including ours, are experimenting with in various ways.

In summary, CORC provides an opportunity for libraries to achieve a long-sought and usually elusive goal: the creation of a true virtual library, with an all-inclusive catalog for each library participant. It also provides an avenue for extending traditional library boundaries, both within and without the library, as non-catalogers engage in building the catalog and librarians seek to engage members of various disciplinary communities in CORC projects. It gives librarians opportunities to participate in leading-edge work in librarianship, in an innovative, highly-visible and challenging effort that can be accomplished by a reordering of priorities. Library administrators have an opportunity to solve a nagging problem–what to do about those collections that remain outside of bibliographic control–while creating new professional growth opportunities for their library faculty members and contributing to a cooperative international effort to establish a reliable and reputable virtual library. There are, of course, many policy and procedural decisions yet to be made and technical issues that will need to be addressed. These are beyond the scope, and expertise, of the authors of this article. What we do already know is that CORC can help us reshape library services and collections.

NOTES

1. Thomas B. Hickey. "CORC–Cooperative Online Resource Catalog," *Annual Review of OCLC Research*, 1998. *http://www.oclc.org/oclc/research/publications/review98/hickey/corc.htm*

2. Paul Duguid. Report of the Santa Fe Planning Workshop on Distributed Knowledge Work Environments: Digital Libraries, March 9-11, 1997 (Ann Arbor: School of Information, University of Michigan). Report version Sept. 20, 1997 *http://www.si.umich.edu/SantaFe*

3. For a review of Z39.50, see Paul Miller. "Z39.50 for All," *Ariadne* no. 21 (Sept. 1999) *http://www.ariadne.ac.uk/issue21/z3950/intro.html*

4. ARL/OCLC Strategic Issues Forum for Academic Library Directors. "The Keystone Principles," 1999. *http://www.arl.org/training/keystone.html*

5. See the Aug. 20 and Nov. 29, 1999 postings regarding health sciences on the CORC-L listserv stored at *http://orc.rsch.oclc.org:5103/corc-l/*

A Relationship Between CORC
and the PCC:
Rationale and Possibilities

John J. Riemer

SUMMARY. The author examines the common purposes of the Program for Cooperative Cataloging (PCC) and the Cooperative Online Resource Catalog (CORC) and offers opinions on the potential relationship and interaction that could exist between them. The future of cooperative cataloging and potential improvements to efficiency are explored. Reflections on the differing natures of the MARC and Dublin Core standards and the interrelationship between them are offered. Finally, CORC-inspired ideas are presented on the leadership role the PCC can offer in the areas of standards, automation, and training. *[Article copies available for a fee from The Haworth Document Delivery Service: 1-800-342-9678. E-mail address: <getinfo@haworthpressinc.com> Website: <http://www.HaworthPress.com>]*

KEYWORDS. Cooperative cataloging, CORC, Program for Cooperative Cataloging, Dublin Core, MARC

INTRODUCTION

Matthew Beacom has remarked that "PCC" and "CORC" both have two C's in them and, in each case, they stand for Cooperative and Catalog(ing).[1]

John J. Riemer serves as the GALILEO CORC Representative and as Assistant Head of Cataloging, University of Georgia Libraries, Athens, GA 30602 (e-mail: jriemer@arches.uga.edu).

[Haworth co-indexing entry note]: "A Relationship Betwen CORC and the PCC: Rationale and Possibilities." Riemer, John J. Co-published simultaneously in *Journal of Internet Cataloging* (The Haworth Information Press, an imprint of The Haworth Press, Inc.) Vol. 4, No. 1/2, 2001, pp. 29-34; and: *CORC: New Tools and Possibilities for Cooperative Electronic Resource Description* (ed: Karen Calhoun, and John J. Riemer) The Haworth Information Press, an imprint of The Haworth Press, Inc., 2001, pp. 29-34. Single or multiple copies of this article are available for a fee from The Haworth Document Delivery Service [1-800-342-9678, 9:00 a.m. - 5:00 p.m. (EST). E-mail address: getinfo@haworthpressinc.com].

That was as good a start as any toward defining an interrelationship between two natural allies.

In its most recent strategic plan, the PCC states its mission as:

> In support of the need to provide access to information resources the Program will seek to cooperatively increase the timely availability of authoritative records created and maintained under accepted standards, to facilitate the cost-effective creation and use of these records, and to provide leadership in the national and international information community.[2]

On its home page, the Cooperative Online Resource Catalog is summarized:

> CORC is a state of the art, Web-based system that helps libraries provide well-guided access to Web resources using new, automated tools and library cooperation. CORC empowers librarians with automated tools for the cooperative creation, selection, organization, and maintenance of web-based resources.[3]

KEEPING UP WITH EVER-INCREASING WORKLOADS

We live in an age when cataloging departments, to stay viable, need to take on the organization of electronic resources This workload comes with few if any additional staff. One of the most memorable moments in an ALA-sponsored metadata institute I attended two years ago was the observation that it simply will not be possible to create a MARC record for every information object on the Web.[4] As Weibel et al. put it, "But current attempts to describe electronic resources according to formal standards (e.g., the TEI header or MARC cataloging) can accom[m]odate only a small subset of the most important resources."[5]

Much like the Core record standard[6] the PCC developed, CORC and the Dublin Core data element set represent a valuable addition to the cataloger's repertoire. CORC can build on and extend the goals and accomplishments of the PCC–particularly, "Quality cataloging records, rich enough in content to be used with little or no modification at the local level and reasonable enough in cost to be generated in large numbers."[7]

Looking first at the cataloging of traditional materials, the ultimate efficiency in first-time cataloging (original or copy cataloging) would be to have everyone join the PCC. Any original cataloging energy expended anywhere ought to be harnessed and the resulting cataloging records included in the program. With a sufficiently broad training effort and subsequent commitment to put the learned skills to use, the quantity of "member copy" could diminish, with a corresponding increase in the amount of the higher-quality PCC copy relished by copy cataloging operations everywhere.

The ultimate efficiency in maintaining the records that have been previously downloaded to individual OPACs would be shifting to a model in which we all catalog in one of the bibliographic utilities that we would all point to from our OPACs. Perform needed maintenance once and you have automatically done it for everyone else's OPAC. In preparation for that day, we will need to develop a sufficient comfort level with each other's records, prepared as they would be according to the standards we have all agreed to follow within our bibliographic community.

Concurrent to the implementation of these efficiencies, CORC brings additional powerful help to our bibliographic control efforts–technology and people. Elsewhere in this volume, Edmunds and Brisson[8] describe some of the powerful record-creation tools the CORC platform offers. The availability of the Dublin Core data element set, designed for use by noncatalogers, together with the ability to crosswalk DC metadata over to MARC records, opens the door wide for additional people to collaborate with existing catalogers. As Calhoun[9] describes, selectors and reference librarians can create and save partial DC records that catalogers can finish in MARC and export to the OPAC. Thanks to the interoperability of metadata, institutions such as archives and museums, often without any catalogers or other librarians on staff, now potentially can create and share their resource descriptions with libraries.

THE INTERPLAY BETWEEN MARC AND OTHER STANDARDS

A dynamic tension exists between the DC and MARC standards. The latter has matured into a detailed, rules-bound standard over the course of 30 years, and it contrasts markedly with the relatively recent arrival whose 15 basic elements are all optional, repeatable, and more subject to varying interpretation.[10]

My role as the GALILEO CORC Representative for the state of Georgia has forced me to think about the relationship between the two standards. I have organized several metadata projects involving the creation of sets of item-level descriptions. In the spirit of utilizing nonlibrarians to create records expeditiously, I attempted in the training to maximize the amount of work done on the Dublin Core side of each record, reserving work on the MARC side for the things that can only be done there. For each project, considerable upfront time goes into analyzing how the available information about the resources fits into the DC data elements, as well as thought about how they ultimately will map to OCLC-MARC and how the resulting records will coexist with others in the OPAC. However, after the initial investment of time required to create the initial couple of records in MARC, the record-cloning capabilities of CORC turn into a very strong asset. Project partici-pants are freed up to focus intellectual energy on what differs from one information object to another. At the same time, a lot of MARC data is carried forward behind the scenes, with negligible effort and minimal obliga-tion for understanding.

PCC LEADERSHIP IN STANDARDS, AUTOMATION, AND TRAINING

Using the PCC standing committee line-up as a guide, a number of tasks suggest themselves as catalogers and other librarians better position them-selves for the digital age. PCC members can monitor and help establish core-level record equivalents in other metadata schemes. They could deter-mine and speak up on the adequacy of data elements in other standards.[11] Similar to the desirability of learning a foreign language, members could both gain familiarity with existing metadata mappings and establish new ones as new schemes come into use, all with an eye toward offering advisory services to a library's clientele.[12]

To extend the model of CORC's metadata harvester to traditional library materials, could publishers be persuaded to share with PCC members the digital source data for the chief sources of publications, and perhaps also the tables of contents? Members ought to pursue with the vendors of automated systems the development of faster editing capabilities; simultaneously, mem-bers ought to develop and systematically share macros and other shortcuts. What improvements could be made in automated (assistance to) classifica-tion? Could the CORC-based URL maintenance service[13] be extended to the Internet addresses that will appear in other types of MARC records, such as authorities? Borrowing from Barbara Tillett's proposal for "access control" by which the view of an authorized name heading can vary internationally,[14] could the various multilingual editions of an electronic publication be de-scribed on a single record whose title proper and parallel titles would display differently in each nation?[15] All of these strategies toward efficiency are insurance against a future need to further retrench the content of the catalog record.

PCC leaders must promote acceptance of the reality that MARC records cannot be created for every information object needing to be cataloged and help guide the discussion that sets the priorities for use of the various levels and tools available to the cataloger. Training needs to be organized and offered in the various additional standards by which one can catalog. How should the training vary, if at all, for the selectors and reference librarians who need to participate in collaborative bibliographic control? What can be done to prepare catalogers to be effective in mapping between metadata standards, designing workflows, preparing instructions, and managing metadata projects?

CONCLUSION

CORC has created a lot of momentum for catalogers and other librarians to accomplish work in new ways. The goals and values and cumulative wisdom of the PCC should inform the use people make of the powerful tools offered by CORC. The PCC program participants should take maximum advantage of the technological improvements and collaborative opportunities CORC can represent. These can and should affect the PCC Tactical Plan[16] for years to come. If the activity recently taking place within CORC participant institutions represents the future of libraries, then managers should strategize to involve as many people as possible, and we should all embrace it.

NOTES

1. Program for Cooperative Cataloging Participants' Meeting, held during annual meeting of the American Library Association, New Orleans, La., June 27, 1999 (author's notes). Formal minutes of the meeting are available from the Library of Congress at <http://lcweb.loc.gov/catdir/pcc/pccpart99a.html>. (All URLs viewed Mar. 12, 2000.) Attribution verified with Matthew Beacom in e-mail of Mar. 13, 2000.

2. Program for Cooperative Cataloging. Strategic Plan, 1997-2002. <http://lcweb.loc.gov/catdir/pcc/stratplan.html>. For a summarization of the benefits of member participation in the PCC, see the final section of Beacher Wiggins, "The Program for Cooperative Cataloging," in Stanley D. Blum, ed. *Proceedings of the Taxonomic Authority Files Workshop, Washington, DC, June 22-23, 1998: A Workshop on the Compilation, Maintenance, and Dissemination of Taxonomic Authority Files (TAF)* (San Francisco, Calif.: California Academy of Sciences, Research Division, 1999) <http://research.calacademy.org/taf/proceedings/wiggins.html>.

3. Cooperative Online Resource Catalog (Dublin, Ohio: OCLC Online Computer Library Center, Inc.) <http://www.oclc.org/oclc/corc/index.htm>. For a listing of CORC's benefits, see the "Reasons to Participate" section of "The OCLC Cooperative Online Resource Catalog Project," <http://www.oclc.org/oclc/promo/10520corc/index.htm>.

4. Managing Metadata for the Digital Library: Crosswalks or Chaos, May 4-5, 1998, Washington, D.C. Sponsored by the American Library Association's Library and Information Technology Association (LITA) and Association for Library Collections & Technical Services (ALCTS).

5. Stuart Weibel, Jean Godby, Eric Miller, Ron Daniel. "OCLC/NCSA Metadata Workshop Report," Mar. 1995 <http://purl.oclc.org/metadata/dublin_core_report>.

6. See first section of Colleen F. Hyslop. "The Core Record and Consolidation of CONSER and PCC." Published in "From Catalog to Gateway," a supplement to the *ALCTS Newsletter* v. 8, no. 4 (1997). Also available: <http://lcweb.loc.gov/catdir/pcc/hyslop2.html>.

7. Program for Cooperative Cataloging. "PCC Values Statement" 1999 <http://lcweb.loc.gov/catdir/pcc/values.html>.

8. Jeff Edmunds and Roger Brisson. "Cataloging in CORC: A Work in Progress," found in this volume.

9. Karen Calhoun, Martha Hsu, Yumin Jiang, Jill Powell, Don Schnedeker, Pam Stansbury, and Bill Walters. "CORC at Cornell Project: Final Report" (Ithaca, N.Y.: Cornell University Libraries, 1999) <http://ivy.mannlib.cornell.edu/corc/corc-final.htm>.

10. For additional observations on the contrasting nature of these two metadata standards, see the CORC database assessment section of Calhoun, et al. <http://ivy.mannlib.cornell.edu/corc/corc-final.htm#corc_db>.

11. See, for example, the paper by Wayne Jones, "Dublin Core and Serials," found in this volume.

12. For example, see the metadata section in "University-Wide Advisory Services Available." *The Harvard University Gazette.* Mar. 25, 1999. <http://www.news.harvard.edu/gazette/1999/03.25/diglibadvise.html> and Robin Wendler's Digital Library Initiative page at <http://hul.harvard.edu/ldi/html/robin_wendler.html>.

13. Matthew Beacom suggested that CORC could help with URL maintenance in PCC records at the PCC Participants' Meeting, New Orleans, La., June 27, 1999 <http://lcweb.loc.gov/catdir/pcc/pccpart99a.html>.

14. For details, see Barbara B. Tillett. "International Shared Resource Records for Controlled Access," in "From Catalog to Gateway," *ALCTS Online Newsletter* v. 10, no. 1 (Dec. 1998). *http://www.ala.org/alcts/alcts_news/v10n1/gateway.html.*

15. For example, see the Bulletin of the European Union's English-language edition web page <http://europa.eu.int/abc/doc/off/bull/en/welcome.htm> which offers links to ten additional online editions in the various other official European languages. Six of the potential 11 cataloging records may be found in the CORC database (OCLC WorldCat ID numbers provided): #38402599 (English), #38750177 (French), #38452438 (German), #38402768 (Italian), #38452579 (Portuguese), and #38452323 (Spanish).

16. Program for Cooperative Cataloging. "PCC Tactical Plan to Support the PCC Strategic Plan, 1998-2002, approved June 25, 1998," updated November 5, 1999 <http://lcweb.loc.gov/catdir/pcc/tacticalplan.html>.

A Faceted Approach to Subject Data in the Dublin Core Metadata Record

Lois Mai Chan
Eric Childress
Rebecca Dean
Edward T. O'Neill
Diane Vizine-Goetz

SUMMARY. The enormous volume and rapid growth of resources available on the World Wide Web and the emergence of numerous metadata schemes have spurred a re-examination of the way subject data is to be provided for Web resources efficiently and effectively. For the Dublin Core metadata record, a new approach to subject vocabulary is being investigated. This new method, called FAST (Faceted Application of Subject Terminology), is based on the existing vocabulary in *Library of Congress Subject Headings* (LC), but applied with a simpler syntax than that currently used by libraries according to Library of Congress application policies. In the FAST system, non-topical (i.e., geographic, chronological, and form) data are separated from topical data and placed in different elements provided in the Dublin Core metadata record. *[Article copies*

Lois Mai Chan is Professor, School of Library and Information Science, University of Kentucky (e-mail: loischan@pop.uky.edu).

Eric Childress is Senior Product Support Specialist, Library Resources Division, OCLC Online Computer Library Center, Inc. (e-mail: eric_childress@oclc.org).

Rebecca Dean is Manager, Authority Control Section, OCLC Online Computer Library Center, Inc. (e-mail: rebecca_dean@oclc.org).

Edward T. O'Neill is Research Scientist, Office of Research, OCLC Online Computer Library Center, Inc. (e-mail: oneill@oclc.org).

Diane Vizine-Goetz is Research Scientist, Office of Research, OCLC Online Computer Library Center, Inc. (e-mail: vizine@oclc.org).

[Haworth co-indexing entry note]: "A Faceted Approach to Subject Data in the Dublin Core Metadata Record." Chan et al. Co-published simultaneously in *Journal of Internet Cataloging* (The Haworth Information Press, an imprint of The Haworth Press, Inc.) Vol. 4, No. 1/2, 2001, pp. 35-47; and: *CORC: New Tools and Possibilities for Cooperative Electronic Resource Description* (ed: Karen Calhoun, and John J. Riemer) The Haworth Information Press, an imprint of The Haworth Press, Inc., 2001, pp. 35-47. Single or multiple copies of this article are available for a fee from The Haworth Document Delivery Service [1-800-342-9678, 9:00 a.m. - 5:00 p.m. (EST). E-mail address: getinfo@haworthpressinc.com].

available for a fee from The Haworth Document Delivery Service: 1-800-342-9678. E-mail address: <getinfo@haworthpressinc.com> Website: <http:// www.HaworthPress.com>]

KEYWORDS. Dublin Core, FAST (Faceted Application of Subject Terminology), LCSH (Library of Congress Subject Headings), metadata, subject analysis

INTRODUCTION

The rapid growth of the Internet and the number of electronic resources now available on the Web have necessitated a re-thinking and re-assessment of the way in which information resources are described and made accessible. The proliferation of metadata schemas and the eagerness with which they are embraced, even before they are fully developed and refined, by various communities are a reflection of the urgent need for new approaches to knowledge organization and maintenance.

Many of the metadata schemas have been developed with specific communities or specific types of resources in mind. Among these schemas, The Dublin Core Initiative is the broadest in scope, attempting to meet the needs of a wide variety of user communities and covering resources in all subject areas and all types of electronic resources.

PREMISE OF DUBLIN CORE

Since its inception, Dublin Core has attracted the attention of various user communities, including libraries, archives, museums, and other information providers. In order to accommodate a wide range of users, the premise of the Dublin Core has been stated in the following terms:

> The Dublin Core is intended to be usable by non-catalogers as well as resource description specialists. (The Dublin Core: A Simple Content Description 1998)

In other words, the intention of Dublin Core is to have a schema that mediates between the unstructured approach to Web resources and the highly sophisticated resource description schemas such as AACR2R/MARC.

The following characteristics distinguish the Dublin Core as a prominent candidate for description of electronic resource: simplicity, semantic interoperability, international consensus, and flexibility (The Dublin Core: A Simple Content Description 1998). To achieve these goals, fifteen elements considered to be essential for the identification and description of Web resources have been defined for the Dublin Core.

One of the fifteen elements in the Dublin Core is designated as SUBJECT (Dublin Core Metadata Element Set: Reference Description 1999):

SUBJECT

> **The topic of the content of the resource.** *Typically, a subject will be expressed as keywords, key phrases or classification codes that describe a topic of the resource. Recommended best practice is to select a value from a controlled vocabulary or formal classification scheme.*

In addition to SUBJECT, a number of other elements in the Dublin Core also contain subject-related or content-related data:

TITLE

DESCRIPTION

TYPE

LANGUAGE

COVERAGE

The definitions of these subject-related elements are set forth in the element-set (Dublin Core Metadata Element Set: Reference Description 1999):

DESCRIPTION

> **An account of the content of the resource.** *Description may include but is not limited to: an abstract, table of contents, reference to a graphical representation of content or a free-text account of the content.*

TYPE

> **The nature or genre of the content of the resource.** *Type includes terms describing general categories, functions, genres, or aggregation levels for content. Recommended best practice is to select a value from a controlled vocabulary.*

LANGUAGE

A language of the intellectual content of the resource. *Recommended best practice for the values of the Language element is defined by RFC 1766, which includes a two-letter Language Code (taken from the ISO 639 standard) followed, optionally, by a two-letter Country Code (taken from the ISO 3166 standard). For example, 'en' for English, 'fr' for French, or 'en-uk' for English used in the United Kingdom.*

COVERAGE

The extent or scope of the content of the resource. *Coverage will typically include spatial location (a place name or geographic coordinates), temporal period (a period label, date, or date range) or jurisdiction (such as a named administrative entity). Recommended best practice is to select a value from a controlled vocabulary (for example, the Thesaurus of Geographic Names) and that, where appropriate, named places or time periods be used in preference to numeric identifiers such as sets of coordinates or date ranges.*

The element *TYPE* constitutes more or less what has been considered traditionally as "form data." Taken together, these content-related elements imply a post-coordinate, faceted approach to content representation. In other words, form, language, place, and time are separate from topical representation in the SUBJECT element. Regrouped, these elements fall into the following categories:

A. Topical description–

SUBJECT

TITLE

DESCRIPTION

B. Form data–

TYPE

C. Language data–

LANGUAGE

D. Spatial or temporal data–

COVERAGE

The Dublin Core has been designed to be extremely flexible; none of the elements is mandatory, and every element is repeatable. In other words, even though there are many elements relating to subject matter, a particular implementation may choose to use all of them or only the *SUBJECT* element for representing content-related data. Each implementation project or agency must define the scope of each element and determine its own policy with regard to the use of these elements.

With regard to the development or adoption of an implementation policy, it is appropriate to consider first the nature of the Web environment for which the Dublin Core has been designed and the functional requirements of a subject access schema for Web resources.

Two of the primary characteristics of Dublin Core Metadata (The Dublin Core: A Simple Content Description 1998) mentioned earlier are particularly pertinent with regard to subject data: simplicity and semantic interoperability. Simplicity refers to the usability by non-catalogers, specifically, to allow the creation of metadata records by persons not necessarily trained in sophisticated methods of bibliographic control. The reason for semantic interoperability is to enable users to search across discipline boundaries and, desirably, also across information retrieval and storage systems.

In keeping with the premises of the Dublin Core, a subject vocabulary suitable for the Web environment has the following functional requirements:

- It should be simple in structure (i.e., easy to assign and use) and easy to maintain;
- It should provide optimal access points;
- It should be flexible and interoperable across disciplines and in various knowledge discovery and access environments, not the least among which is the OPAC.

PREVIOUS EFFORTS TO REVISE LIBRARY OF CONGRESS SUBJECT HEADINGS (LCSH)

The complexity of LCSH has prompted several simplification attempts. Among these, the Subject Subdivisions Conference, also known as the Airlie Conference (The Future of Subdivisions 1992), attempted to simplify the application of LCSH subdivisions. At that conference, many of the problems associated with LCSH subdivision practice were identified and a series of recommendations were made, including the following:

- A standard order of subdivision (topical, geographic, chronological, and form) should be used for topical headings;
- The use of free-floating subdivisions should be expanded;

- Chronological subdivisions should reflect the actual time period covered in the work.

Since the Airlie Conference, the Library of Congress has embarked on a series of efforts to simplify subdivision practice. Nonetheless, the pre-coordinated string remains.

In 1997, an ALCTS/SAC/Subcommittee on Metadata and Subject Analysis was established with the following charge: *Identify and study the major issues surrounding the use of metadata in the subject analysis and classification of digital resources. Provide discussion forums and programs relevant to these issues.* The Subcommittee did an excellent job of analyzing the needs for the subject analysis of digital resources. It started with the assumption that the schema must be simple, easy to apply, intuitive, scalable, logical, and appropriate to the specific discipline of implementation. Unlike the Airlie Conference, the Subcommittee focused on identifying different approaches to subject data rather than on enhancing LCSH.

The Subcommittee concluded that using a mixture of keywords and controlled vocabulary is the most viable approach for digital resources. The potential sources of controlled vocabulary include:

- Use existing schema(s);
- Adapt or modify existing schema(s);
- Develop new schema(s).

For a general vocabulary covering all subjects, members of the Subcommittee considered two options: *(1) Using LCSH subject strings, if possible (i.e., if time and trained personnel are available), particularly in the OPAC environment or (2) Breaking up LCSH strings to topic, place, period, language, etc., and using other Dublin Core elements (type, coverage) in addition to the SUBJECT element.* They recommended the second option, the use of *separate elements for form, chronology, type, time, and space, particularly in situations where non-catalogers are involved in the creation of metadata records.*

IMPLEMENTING SUBJECT ELEMENT IN THE CORC PROJECT

The CORC (Cooperative Online Resource Catalog) Project, initiated by OCLC in 1998, seeks to test an experimental model for the implementation of the Dublin Core, which may eventually develop into a working tool. The subject analysis requirements for CORC are very similar to those identified by the ALCTS/SAC/Subcommittee but with additional emphasis on: (1) compatibility between any new schema and LCSH, and (2) amenability to automated authority control.

Two key decisions are required to create a new subject schema: defining the semantics (the choice of vocabulary) and the syntax (pre-coordination vs. post-coordination). Regarding the semantics, OCLC decided to retain LCSH vocabulary. CORC participants are expected to continue to apply LCSH, even if a new schema becomes available and widely accepted. By adapting the LCSH vocabulary, the compatibility with LCSH is retained. As a subject vocabulary, LCSH offers several advantages:

- It is a rich vocabulary covering all subject areas, easily the largest general indexing vocabulary in the English language;
- There is synonym and homograph control;
- It contains rich links (cross references) among terms;
- LCSH is a de facto universal controlled vocabulary and has been translated or adapted as a model for developing subject heading systems by many countries around the world;
- It is compatible with subject data in MARC records;
- With a common vocabulary, automated conversion of LCSH to the new schema is possible;
- The cost of maintaining the new schema is minimized since many of the changes to LCSH can be incorporated into the new schema.

While LCSH has served users of OPACs long and well, its complex pre-coordinate syntax poses significant disadvantages:

- Because of its complex syntax and rules, the application of LCSH requires highly trained personnel;
- Subject heading strings in bibliographic or metadata records are costly to maintain;
- The syntax of LCSH is not compatible with most other controlled vocabularies;
- It is not amenable to search engines outside of the OPAC environment, particularly current Web search engines; and,
- Due to the complex rules for constructing headings, authority control is of limited effectiveness.

While the rich vocabulary and semantic relationships in LCSH provide subject access beyond the capabilities of keywords, its complex syntax presents a stumbling block and runs counter to the basic premises of simplicity and semantic operability of the Dublin Core. The preferred solution is to devise a simplified syntax using the LCSH vocabulary. The resulting schema would have a controlled vocabulary based on the terminology and relationships already established in LCSH but structured with a different syntax and applied with different policies and procedures that are more inclined towards post-coordination. One of the advantages of such an approach is that, by separating syntax from semantics, the syntax can be simplified while the richness of vocabulary in LCSH is retained, making the schema easier to use and maintain.

The central issue involving the syntax of a controlled vocabulary is pre-coordination vs. post-coordination. Both have precedence in cataloging and indexing practice. Subject vocabularies used in MARC records are typically pre-coordinated subject heading strings, while controlled vocabularies used in online databases are mostly single-concept descriptors, relying on post-coordination for complex subjects. The structure of the elements in the Dublin Core, as discussed earlier, implies or at least allows a faceted, post-coordinate approach. For the sake of simplicity and semantic interoperability, the post-coordinate approach is more in line with the basic premises and characteristics of the Dublin Core. It is in keeping with the primary intent of the Dublin Core to make it "usable by non-catalogers as well as by those with experience with formal resource description models."

Although there is an LCSH authority file that contains established headings, its primary coverage is for the roots of constructed subject headings. Only about three percent of all of the topical headings in WorldCat match authority records–the remaining headings were formed by subdividing the established forms. The rules for constructing a heading are complex–the *Subject Cataloging Manual: Subject Headings* (*Subject Cataloging Manual* 1996) contains four volumes of complex guidelines. The correct construction of subject headings requires extensive education–typically at least two graduate level courses–and years of experience. Since many CORC users are not expected to be skilled subject catalogers, automated authority control must play a significant role to ensure the quality of the subjects assigned. The application rules could be greatly simplified by fully establishing all headings in the new schema, thus eliminating most of the rules for heading construction and greatly simplifying authority control.

THE FAST SUBJECT SCHEMA

After analyzing the requirements of the Dublin Core and reviewing the previous attempts to improve LCSH or to provide other schema for metadata, OCLC is developing a Faceted Application of Subject Terminology (FAST) schema derived from the Library of Congress Subject Headings. The FAST schema is:

- Based on the LCSH vocabulary;
- Designed for an online environment;
- A post-coordinated faceted vocabulary;

- Usable by people with minimal training and experience, and
- Compatible with authority control.

Facets

FAST is being developed in two phases. The first phase includes the development of facets based on the vocabulary found in LCSH topical and geographic headings. The sources of the four distinct types of subfields (facets) that are used in topical and geographic headings are shown in Table 1. Initially, FAST will be limited to these four facets. In a later phase of development, it is anticipated that additional facets will be added for personal names, corporate names, conference/meetings, uniform titles and name-title entries. With the exception of the period facet, all FAST headings will be established in an authority file.

Topical headings will consist of topical main headings and their corresponding general subdivisions and general subdivisions from geographic headings. Period subdivisions with topical aspects will be considered to be both general and period subdivisions for the purpose of FAST. The FAST topical headings look very similar to the established form of LCSH topical headings with the exception that all free-floating topical subdivisions will be part of the established form of the heading and all multiple subdivisions will be expanded. However, rather than establishing all possible combinations, only those that have actually been used will be established. For example, headings based on the multiple

Abortion–Religious aspects–Buddhism, [Christianity, etc.]

will be established only with the religions used–not with all known religions.

TABLE 1. Facets

Facet	Source	MARC codes
Topical	Topical term and general subdivisions from topical headings, the general subdivisions from geographic headings, and period subdivisions which have topical aspects.	650 a & x; 651 x; selected 650 & 651 y
Geographic	Name from geographic headings and the geographic subdivisions from topical headings	650 z; 651 a & z
Period	Chronological subdivisions	650 y; 651 y
Form	Form subdivisions	*650 v; 651 v*

All geographic names will be established and used in indirect order, **Ohio–Columbus** rather than in direct order, **Columbus (Ohio)**. In LCSH, names used as main headings are entered in direct order but when used as subdivisions they appear in indirect form. As in LCSH, a hierarchical name structure will be used. However, unlike LCSH, the first level geographic names will be limited to names from the *USMARC Code List for Geographic Areas* table (USMARC Code List 1998). The number of names that can be used as first level entries in LCSH is far greater than the number of names in the *Geographic Area Codes* table. For example, LC has established some relatively obscure names like **Morgan line** (sh 85-87259) as first level entries. Since the Morgan line–the boundary line drawn from Trieste to the Austrian frontier dividing Italy from Yugoslavia during the post-War occupation–spans national boundaries, it does not require qualification in LCSH. However, in FAST, it would be entered indirectly under Europe, the smallest first level area in which it is fully contained. The resulting FAST entry would be **Europe–Morgan line**. Associating each first level entry with a Geographic Area Code will facilitate the development of search features that use the hierarchical structure of geographic names in FAST. A typical portion of the geographic area code table is shown in Table 2.

The difficulty of working with geographic names can be illustrated with an example: a search of WorldCat for the name Charlevoix produces results that include the use of the name as a city, a lake, a county in Michigan, and two counties in Québec. A WorldCat search identified the 47 different geographic entries shown in alphabetical order in the left column in Figure 1. However, there are actually only 19 distinct geographic entities as shown in the right column. Many of the entities, such as **Charlevoix (Mich.)** and **Michigan–Charlevoix**, result from using different forms of the same name to generate direct and indirect entries. Others, such as **Québec (Province)–Charlevoix** and **Québec–Charlevoix**, result from inconsistent qualifi-

TABLE 2. Geographic Areas Codes

Norway [e-no]	Oceania [po]
Norwegian Sea	UF
Assigned code:	Oceanica
[ln]	Oceania, French
North Atlantic Ocean	USE
Nova Scotia [n-cn-ns]	French Polynesia
Nyasaland	Oceanica
USE	USE
Malawi	Oceania
Ocean Island (Kiribati)	**Ohio [n-us-oh]**
USE	**Ohio River [n-uso]**
Banaba	

FIGURE 1. LCSH vs. FAST Geographic Names

Geographic Names from LCSH	FAST Geographic Names
Charlevoix (Mich.)	Michigan–Charlevoix
Charlevoix (Quebec)	Michigan–Charlevoix County
Charlevoix County (Mich.)	Michigan–Charlevoix County–Beaver Island
Charlevoix County (Quebec)	Michigan–Charlevoix County–Deer Creek Watershed
Charlevoix Harbor (Mich.)	Michigan–Charlevoix County–Holy Island
Charlevoix Region (Mich.)	Michigan–Charlevoix County–Horton Creek
Charlevoix Region (Quebec)	Michigan–Charlevoix County–Horton Creek Marsh
Charlevoix Site (Mich.)	Michigan–Charlevoix County–Marion
Charlevoix, Lake (Mich.)	Michigan–Charlevoix County–O'Neill Site
Charlevoix-Est (Quebec : Regional	Michigan–Charlevoix County–Peaine Township
County Municipality)	Michigan–Charlevoix County–St. James Township
Charlevoix-Est (Quebec)	Michigan–Charlevoix Harbor
Charlevoix-Est County (Que.)	Michigan–Charlevoix Region
Charlevoix-Est County (Quebec)	Michigan–Charlevoix Site
Charlevoix-Ouest (Quebec)	Michigan–Lake Charlevoix
Charlevoix-Ouest County (Que.)	Quebec–Charlevoix Region
Charlevoix-Ouest County (Quebec)	Quebec–Charlevoix-Est
Clermont (Charlevoix-Est, Quebec)	Quebec–Charlevoix-Est–Clermont
Deer Creek Watershed (Charlevoix	Quebec–Charlevoix-Ouest
County, Mich.)	
Holy Island (Charlevoix County, Mich.)	
Horton Creek (Charlevoix County, Mich.)	
Horton Creek Marsh (Charlevoix County,	
Mich.)	
Lake Charlevoix (Mich.)	
Lake Charlevoix (Michigan)	
Marion (Charlevoix County, Mich.)	
Michigan–Beaver Island (Charlevoix	
County)	
Michigan–Charlevoix	
Michigan–Charlevoix County	
Michigan–Charlevoix Region	
Michigan–Charlevoix, Lake	
Michigan–Deer Creek Watershed	
(Charlevoix County)	
Michigan–Horton Creek (Charlevoix	
County)	
Michigan–Lake Charlevoix	
Michigan–Marion (Charlevoix County)	
Michigan–Peaine Township	
(Charlevoix County)	
Michigan–St. James Township (Charlevoix	
County)	
O'Neill Site, Charlevoix County (Mich.)	
Quebec (Province)–Charlevoix	
Quebec (Province)–Charlevoix Co.	
Quebec (Province)–Charlevoix East	
Quebec (Province)–Charlevoix Region	
Quebec (Province)–Charlevoix West	
Quebec (Province)–Charlevoix-Est	
Quebec (Province)–Charlevoix-Est	
(Regional County Municipality)	
Quebec (Province)–Charlevoix-Ouest	
Quebec–Charlevoix Region	
Quebec–Charlevoix-Est	
Quebec–Charlevoix-Ouest	

cation. Abbreviations and inverted forms are other common sources of duplicate names for the same entity. Furthermore, a bigger problem is the
difficulty in displaying the direct and indirect forms of the names together.
Without reformatting the headings, logical clustering is impossible.

In FAST, all geographic names are represented in indirect order. There is
no limit on the number of levels, although the need for more than three levels
appears rare. Qualifiers will only be used to identify the type of geographic
name (Kingdom, Satellite, Duchy, Princely State, etc.). It is expected that this
simplified notation will lead to clearer displays as seen in the right column of
Figure 1.

Form subdivisions will be treated as another distinct facet. The initial set
of form headings will be identified by extracting form subdivisions from
LCSH topical and geographic headings. Form subdivisions are currently
coded both x and v in LCSH headings in WorldCat. Those coded x will be
algorithmically identified and re-coded as v. The algorithm, developed by
OCLC, for identifying form headings will be described in detail in a forthcoming paper.

Period headings for FAST will follow the practice recommended at the
Airlie Conference: Chronological headings will reflect the actual time period
of coverage for the resource. All period headings will be expressed as either a
single numeric date or as a date range. For example, the default time period
associated with the period, **Wars of the Huguenots, 1562-1598**, would be
1562 to 1598. However, in reducing this subdivision to simply a date range,
the name of the war is lost. To prevent this loss of information, period
subdivisions with topical aspects will also be treated as general subdivisions
under the main heading. For example, the subdivision **Wars of the Huguenots, 1562-1598** would be treated as if it had been entered as the general
subdivision **Wars of the Huguenots, 1562-1598** and the period subdivision
1562-1598, ensuring that both the chronological and topical aspects are retained in the appropriate facet. Further, since a period heading should reflect
the actual time period covered, for a work covering only a single battle, e.g.,
one that occurred in 1565, the period heading would be limited to that single
year.

Creation of FAST Authority Files

The initial FAST authority files will be built by faceting LCSH headings
from WorldCat. For example the following LCSH heading,

> ***France $x History $y Wars of the Huguenots, 1562-1598 $v Juvenile
> literature***

would result in the following FAST headings:

Topical:	**History–Wars of the Huguenots, 1562-1598**
Geographic:	**France**
Period:	**1562-1598**
Form:	**Juvenile literature.**

A file containing all unique Library of Congress topical and geographic subject headings in WorldCat has been created. This file contains 6,912,980 unique topical and 1,471,023 geographic headings, representing over 50 million individual subject heading assignments. These headings will be faceted to create the initial versions of the FAST topical, geographic, and form authority files.

These initial versions of the FAST authorities will undergo extensive validation to minimize the number of erroneous entries. The entries remaining after this validation step will be established as FAST subject headings. The final step in creating the FAST authority files will be the addition of cross-references, notes, and other similar information necessary to convert established heading to an authority record.

CONCLUSION

Providing subject data in the CORC metadata record presents both a challenge and an opportunity to explore new approaches to subject analysis and access to electronic resources and to test the viability of an existing subject vocabulary (LCSH in this case) in the Web environment. The purpose of adapting the LCSH with a simplified syntax in CORC is to retain the very rich vocabulary of LCSH while making the schema easier to maintain, apply, and use.

REFERENCES

The Dublin Core: A Simple Content Description Model for Electronic Resources: Metadata for Electronic Resources. (1998). (http://purl.org/DC/index.htm)

Dublin Core Metadata Element Set: Reference Description. (1999). (http://purl.oclc. org/dc/documents/rec-dces-19990702.htm)

The Future of Subdivisions in the Library of Congress Subject Headings System: Report from the Subject Subdivisions Conference Sponsored by the Library of Congress, May 9-12, 1991, edited by Martha O'Hara Conway. Washington, DC: Cataloging Distribution Service, Library of Congress, 1992.

Subject Cataloging Manual: Subject Headings. 5th ed. Prepared by the Cataloging Policy and Support Office, Library of Congress. Washington, D.C.: Cataloging Distribution Service, Library of Congress, 1996-.

USMARC Code List for Geographic Areas. Prepared by the Library of Congress Network Development and MARC Standards Office. Web Version of 1998 Edition. (http://lcweb.loc.gov/marc/geoareas/)

Terminology Identification
in a Collection of Web Resources

Carol Jean Godby
Ray Reighart

SUMMARY. The primary goal of the WordSmith project is to obtain subject terminology directly from raw text. We are currently investigating the hypothesis that reliable subject terms can be automatically collected, re-used, and organized into thesaurus-like objects that enhance access to material that is unwieldy to classify by hand, such as the Web documents in the CORC database. Baseline results of our work are already visible in the CORC project. Catalogers who check the *Generate possible subject terms* button in the process of creating a description for a new item may retrieve novel subject terms, such as *animal genome databases, backcountry Web sites, digital communities, e-mail viruses,* and *worldwide Internet music.* These terms are too new to appear in standard library classification schemes. In later versions of CORC, we want to make automatic keyword assignment more responsive to the needs of catalogers and use this terminology in other ways to increase subject access to the CORC collection. Our paper describes the current

Carol Jean Godby is a Senior Research Scientist at OCLC. She has worked on a variety of projects involving full-text databases, electronic publishing, information retrieval, the Dewey Decimal Classification, metadata, and natural language processing. She is currently managing a project whose goal is to incorporate natural language processing solutions into OCLC's database products. She is a PhD candidate in linguistics at the Ohio State University (e-mail: godby@oclc.org).

Ray Reighart is a Senior Systems Analyst at OCLC. His specialty is computational linguistics and Java programming, and he has developed much of the software in the WordSmith project. He has a PhD in physics from Ohio University (e-mail: reighart@oclc.org).

[Haworth co-indexing entry note]: "Terminology Identification in a Collection of Web Resources." Godby, Carol Jean, and Ray Reighart. Co-published simultaneously in *Journal of Internet Cataloging* (The Haworth Information Press, an imprint of The Haworth Press, Inc.) Vol. 4, No. 1/2, 2001, pp. 49-65; and: *CORC: New Tools and Possibilities for Cooperative Electronic Resource Description* (ed: Karen Calhoun, and John J. Riemer) The Haworth Information Press, an imprint of The Haworth Press, Inc., 2001, pp. 49-65. Single or multiple copies of this article are available for a fee from The Haworth Document Delivery Service [1-800-342-9678, 9:00 a.m. - 5:00 p.m. (EST). E-mail address: getinfo@haworthpressinc.com].

49

implementation of WordSmith in CORC, an evaluation of the results, and proposed future enhancements. *[Article copies available for a fee from The Haworth Document Delivery Service: 1-800-342-9678. E-mail address: <getinfo@haworthpressinc.com> Website: <http://www.HaworthPress.com>]*

KEYWORDS. WordSmith, automatic keyword assignment, terminology, subject analysis, CORC, computational linguistics

AUTOMATED METADATA EXTRACTION IN THE CORC PROJECT

About eighteen months ago, Thomas Hickey, OCLC's chief scientist and director of the CORC project, asked:

> What needs to be cataloged on the Web? The short answer is *too much.* Current estimates of the Web are so large as to make the task of cataloging every page on it nearly impossible, and even the material that deserves to be cataloged will stretch libraries' capabilities. (Hickey 1998)

The developers of the CORC software are addressing this problem by automating much of the work required to create metadata records of Web resources. Many of the important fields in a CORC record can be obtained from the HTTP transaction that is initiated when the user signals an intention to catalog a particular Web page, including the title, author, publisher, URL, date issued, data format, summaries, and keywords. This information makes a good start to a high-quality catalog record, but it satisfies only minimal standards, at best, and it is not always present or reliably coded. Several research projects at OCLC are attempting to contribute to the automated creation of metadata records by gathering information that is more abstract than can be obtained by the parsing of literal fields in a transaction record or HTML record. Examples include language identification, the assignment of subjects from standard classification schemes, and the extraction of keywords or index terms in Web pages that lack a <META> tag.

Here we will report on the contribution of the WordSmith research project to CORC. The primary goal of the WordSmith research project is to automatically identify significant subject terminology in machine-readable text. In experimental implementations of the CORC software, WordSmith is invoked when the cataloger issues a command to *generate possible subject terms.* The result is a set of keywords obtained from the Web document of interest which the cataloger may edit and add to the descriptive record as uncontrolled vocabulary or to the MARC 690 field. In this paper, we describe how the

keywords are identified in unstructured text, how keyword extraction interacts with other abstract processes for automatically identifying metadata, and
how the results may be evaluated and improved with input from human
judges.

SUBJECT TERMINOLOGY FROM SOURCE DOCUMENTS

We believe that terminology identified from source documents will supplement the controlled vocabulary obtained from thesauri and library classification schemes and provide another point of access to textual databases.
Terminology obtained directly from text is more comprehensive and timely
than that found in a hand-built resource but also far more noisy. A major
focus of our research project is to identify ways to distinguish idiosyncratic
expression from stable and long-lasting terminology.

Our experiments to date have shown that the results from the WordSmith
terminology extraction software may be in the same style or level of general-
ity as the vocabulary of standard library classification schemes (Vizine-Goetz
and Godby 1997). For example, the phrases *grey holes*, *lunar eclipses* and
triple stars were extracted from a collection of popular articles about astrono-
my and could supplement the index terms *black holes*, *solar eclipses* and
double stars found in Edition 21 of the Dewey Decimal Classification
(Mitchell 1996). As another example, many CORC records have keywords,
usually obtained from the Library of Congress Subject Headings, that indicate the genre of the resources described in the Web document, such as
databases, *catalogues*, *electronic information resources*, *directories*, and
computer network resources. To this list, WordSmith processes applied to
CORC records can add *information catalog services*, *government news sites*,
online services catalog, *personal papers*, *documents and photographs*, and
socioeconomic data and applications.

Perhaps more important is the theoretical possibility that terminology
extracted from full-text resources can genuinely add to the information found
in lists of controlled vocabulary. It can be supplemental for the following
reasons:

- *Novelty.* A software program that can mine terminology directly from
  hundreds of megabytes of text can document cultural novelty much
  more quickly than human editors. The records in the CORC database
  point to a universe that mostly did not exist even five years ago, featur-
  ing *backcountry Web sites*, *bread machine bread*, *digital communities*,
  e-mail viruses, *Internet radio*, *eBay*, *Cyber Café*, and *metadata creation
  tools*. None of these phrases or proper names have yet appeared in the
  Dewey Decimal Classification or the Library of Congress Subject
  Headings.

- *Specificity.* Terminology from source documents supplements standard subject headings with detail that might increase the precision of a database search. For example, a CORC record containing the LCSH heading *oil spills–Environmental aspects* contains the following more specific phrases extracted by WordSmith: *Sea Empress oil spill, Crude oil pollution, Oil spill Web sites,* and *Oil pollution incidents in European history.* Similarly, a CORC record with the LCSH heading *Strategic materials–Middle East* points to a Web site containing the phrases *military trends, Arab-Israeli military balance, Security trends in Iran,* and *Overview of military build-up in Iraq.*
- *Linguistic currency.* Because the language of controlled vocabularies is standardized, it may often sound unnatural or stilted to users who are not trained catalogers. One of the research objectives defined by Forest Press, the publisher of the Dewey Decimal Classification, is to include more vocabulary that is closer to the language of casual users, increasing its utility as a browsing and searching tool for online resources (Vizine-Goetz 1998b). Some of our work with WordSmith supports this effort. In experiments with terminology extraction from news sources, we were able to offer *auto insurance* as an alternative to the Dewey Decimal Classification captions *Motor Vehicle Insurance* and *automobile insurance*; *health plan(s)* to *Health Insurance*; and *flat tax* to the LCSH phrase *flat-rate income tax.*

THE AUTOMATIC IDENTIFICATION
OF SUBJECT TERMINOLOGY

As we said in Godby and Reighart (1998, 1999), our work focuses on phrases that are functionally similar to words. Our analysis does not exclude the consideration of single words, but in most subjects, especially technical subjects that are undergoing rapid evolution, phrases are far more common and less ambiguous. Witness the preponderance of phrases in the science and technology sections of the Relative Index in the Dewey Decimal Classification.

We usually think of a phrase as a momentary description, a reflex of every human's ability to construct unique expressions that have never been heard or seen before. Linguists refer to these as *syntactic phrases*, and any text is full of them. For example, this paper, for better or worse, has the syntactic phrases *the consideration of single words, language of controlled vocabularies*, and *terminology from source documents*. Though most phrases are quickly created and forgotten, a small number are more stable. Like words, they are listed in dictionaries, indexes, and translations, signalling that they are no longer an individual's unique property, but shared by a community of speakers. As a reminder of their word-like status, some of them may even be eventually written as single words or acronyms. For example, only archaic texts mention *data bases*. Structured, searchable collections of information are now referred to as *databases*, or simply *DBs*, by computer people.

The linguist Hans Marchand, an expert on the subject of English word formation, calls the phrases that are of interest to us *lexical phrases* (Marchand 1969: 80). Like words, useful lexical phrases give convenient names to things or concepts that are salient in a speaker's experience and imply the existence of something persistent or habitual. The linguist Pamela Downing (1975) makes these points with the noun phrase *garbage man*. As she says, not everyone who handles garbage is a garbage man, only those who do this job for a living. Evidence for the word-like properties of *garbage man* can also be measured. For one thing, this phrase is relatively frequent and highly stable. Plausible and comprehensible alternative expressions, such as *person who takes away the garbage, trash man, garbage hauler, trash person,* or *garbage guy,* are uncommon and are perhaps the hallmark of non-native English. *Garbage man* is also in general usage among American English speakers, appearing in the writing and speech of many authors as well as in some dictionaries and translations.

As linguists have observed, lexical phrases such as *garbage man* are noun-noun compounds because they are noun phrases that consist of sequences of nouns. If all lexical phrases were noun-noun compounds, the computational task of recognizing them would be relatively easy because sequences of nouns that are not nominal compounds are otherwise uncommon in English, appearing only occasionally in infelicitous sentences such as *She gave her dog biscuits.* But linguists have argued that many adjective-noun combinations such as *black market* and *electrical engineer* are also lexical phrases because they are linguistically stable and name persistent concepts. So are some noun phrases containing prepositions or conjunctions, such as *mother of pearl* or *bread and butter,* and so are some entire sentences, such as *kiss me under the garden gate,* the name of a flower in Grandma's garden.

Our research problem is to find the optimal combination of structural and distributional criteria that distinguish lexical from syntactic phrases. If attention is restricted to noun-noun compounds, too many lexical phrases are excluded; if other kinds of phrases are considered, statistical measures such as frequency must be engaged to filter out what are mostly syntactic phrases. We must rely on such criteria because a lexical phrase involves a relationship between language and a persistent object or concept in the speaker's world, which is not directly measurable. Our hypothesis is that there are traces in the written record and that these can be good enough to make the sought-after distinction.

So far, we have relied heavily on the following heuristics to identify lexical phrases:

- Include simple noun phrases such as single nouns, adjective-noun phrases and noun-noun compounds but exclude those with subordinate clauses, such as *the kind of disequilibrium that many scientists fear.* We are evaluating the suitability of noun phrases with prepositional phrases and conjunctions.
- Include noun phrases that are internally stable and highly frequent. Godby and Reighart (1999) describe the algorithms that we use to measure stability.
- Include noun phrases that share a common rightmost member or 'head.' Several computational linguists have observed that a coherent document that develops a single subject often has noun phrases clustered around a small number of common head nouns (Wacholder 1998, Nakegawa and Kori 1998). For example, a news article about air pressure on Mars contains the noun phrases *planet*, *earthlike planet*, *air pressure*, *atmospheric pressure*, and *sea-level pressure.*
- Exclude noun phrases with certain modifiers. Noun phrases starting with *this*, *that*, *such*, *previous*, *corresponding*, or *respective* usually depend on the surrounding language of the text and are excluded because we are interested in phrases that retain their meaning even when they are taken out of particular texts. Noun phrases containing certain words that indicate an individual speaker's attitude or opinion are also eliminated, such as *very interesting* subject or *daunting* problem, because lexical phrases are, by definition, used by an entire community of speakers to refer to the same object or concept.

The automatic identification of lexical phrases is still a research topic, as we are reminded as we witness our colleagues at OCLC grapple with the difficult technical, cultural–and even linguistic–issues of metadata on the Internet. Because they are defining a new subject, they are under great pressure to name all of those concepts they have introduced, creating expressions that can be shared among other members of their community and eventually introduced to outsiders who benefit from their work. The articles from the Metadata research community, such as those on the Dublin Core Web site (Dublin Core 1999), illustrate why software like WordSmith is important for cataloging and indexing tasks: they are full of novelty, specificity, and linguistic currency.

As observant linguists, we can be reasonably certain that these documents contain a new sense of the word *metadata* and the new lexical phrase *Dublin Core* because these have made it into translations (Koch 1998), the Dewey Decimal Classification, and even Yahoo's subject taxonomy *Computers and*

Internet > Information and Documentation > Metadata > Dublin Core. But when the WordSmith software is applied to documents on the Dublin Core Web site, the result is an abundance of noun phrases that pass most of the tests for lexical phrases discussed above. Table 1 shows some examples.

Are all of these lexical phrases? It's hard to tell from a superficial look because they may be persistent names, but names of such obscure objects in the Metadata universe that only the most engaged experts would know what they refer to. Or they may be idiosyncratic descriptions of one or two writers, or phrases that our software has parsed incorrectly.

The WordSmith software works in slightly different ways depending on whether the lexical phrases are extracted from individual documents or from collections. Though both are necessary for products at OCLC that create indexes of full-text databases, the more pressing need in the CORC project is for processes that work on single documents because users focus on one document at a time. Many of the heuristics mentioned above work on individual documents, such as those that look for noun phrases, identify and cluster them according to their head words, or exclude noun phrases with certain modifiers such as *very*.

What can't be done very well on individual documents are the measures of frequency and stability that distinguish an individual's writing style from common usage. In addition, it is possible to correct some parsing errors in larger texts or document collections, but not in the single, sparsely worded documents that are typical of the Web title pages or home pages that are the focus of interest for many contributors to the CORC project. Thus, if lexical phrase candidates like those in Table 1 were taken from a large collection, it would be possible to determine with reasonable confidence that *educational qualifiers* and *metadata-aware Web browsers* and *element format label* are names for persistent concepts, that *core qualifiers* and *library of congress*

TABLE 1. Some lexical phrase candidates from Web documents about metadata.

basic core elements	discovery infrastructure
automatic RDF metadata generator	educational qualifiers
clarification of element definition removal	element format label
Australian Government Locator Service	global crawler services
canonical elements	resource
catalog of Internet resources	metadata exchange capabilities
collection management and resource discovery	metadata-aware Web browsers
core qualifiers	rights management label
DC date subelements	object genres
digital document metadata	RDF model and syntax specification
Library of Congress subject	namespace name
categories of types	descriptive standards
element format label	multimedia resource base

subject are incorrect parses, and that *clarification of element definition removal* is the expression of a single writer.

AN EVALUATION

To make further progress on the problem of automated terminology identification, we need a study with human judges. Our software uses heuristics to identify potentially valuable terminology, but it must be double-checked because it represents only an educated guess. There is an inescapable human element because the terminology that our software extracts must ultimately be familiar, natural, and useful. A second reason is that we are interested in evaluating the performance of the version of WordSmith that identifies subject terminology in individual documents. Perhaps for some uses, such as the assignment of subject terms to CORC records as part of the workflow in a cataloging session, the process must be human-mediated, but we need to make sure that the data extracted is as good as possible and is at least minimally useful. Results from this very difficult test of our software also promise to improve other applications of WordSmith in CORC that are more automated, such as the preprocessing of a document for automatic subject assignment, or the indexing of document collections. We will briefly discuss these uses in Section 5 of this paper.

In the rest of this paper, we report on a study that simulates one of the uses of WordSmith in the CORC project: given a Web page, WordSmith extracts words and phrases. The reviewer decides whether they are good or poor subject descriptors. CORC participants supplied the judgments.

Page Selection

One hundred URLs were randomly selected from the complete set of 197,862 URLs for Web pages that had records in the CORC database as of September 30, 1999. These Web pages were harvested. Candidates for further processing by the WordSmith terminology extraction software were eliminated using the criteria shown in Table 2.

All potential failures, except the first, can be detected automatically. A page was judged to have unstable content if it contained an *Under Construction* message or if it consisted of obviously dated material, such as the front page of a newspaper or magazine. Concepts could be extracted from such pages but they would have little value in a collection of the persistent Internet resources that the CORC project is intended to represent. Pages that were smaller than 2K were judged to have too little text. These were usually directory pages that consisted of a series of links or cover pages containing a

TABLE 2. Modes of failure for page selection.

Unstable content	2
Text is too sparse	18
Not HTML or HTTP	16
The page has moved	2
Broken links	32
Potential candidates	30
Total:	100

dominant image and a brief instruction to go forward. Concepts could be extracted from these pages, too, but they are not meaningful for the purposes of the current experiment because we are interested in the performance of heuristics for selecting and ranking potential subject terminology, and the output from such pages is often trivially short.

In the remaining modes of failure, no terminology can be extracted. Resources that did not contain HTML were eliminated because we could not guarantee that they contained text. Such resources often consist of directory listings that present the same problems for content analysis as URLs. File and directory names are often meaningful and can perhaps be parsed, but this task is currently beyond the scope of our project. The last two problems are more worrisome for the CORC project. Obviously, they are not a limitation of our software because the URLs must have been valid when the CORC record was created. Many broken links had HTML page names containing numbers, possibly indicating that they were automatically generated and had changing content, as on a news site; or they contained the tilde (~) character, suggesting that they resided in a personal home directory; or they referred to Port 80, the publicly accessible port on standard HTTP installations that is often used as a temporary directory. The study of URL failures deserves a separate paper, but observations like these might help us understand which Web sites deserve closer attention by the library community.

The numbers in Table 2 give one strong hint as to why the automatic generation of subject metadata is not mature in the current implementation of the CORC project. In fact, 30% is an overestimate of the candidate pages suitable for concept extraction by WordSmith because it is based only on file size. Additional pages had to be eliminated because they were too sparse after filtering out large amounts of stylistic HTML markup, blocks of program code delimited by Javascript or Style tags, and bona-fide text in languages other than English. After these pages were eliminated, the list of Web pages from which concepts can be extracted is reduced to less than 20%. All of the problems discussed here limit the effectiveness not only of WordSmith but also of automatic subject assignment, which, as currently implemented in experimental versions of CORC, uses an enriched version of the Dewey Decimal Classification (Vizine-Goetz 2000).

Nevertheless, we are confident that many of the obstacles can be overcome. Software is being written at OCLC that automatically manages URLs, tracking those that change location. Some of the failures with the implementations of the terminology extraction and automatic subject assignment features currently available in the CORC software can be attributed to immature versions of HTML parsers, which are now being refined. As for the pages with sparse text and non-HTML content, automatic metadata extraction is often accurate but uninteresting. They might be more valuable if based on the contents of the resources usually linked to such pages. OCLC already has proven technology to accommodate the necessary change in design for the retrieval of Web pages in the CORC record creation workflow. The harvester can be configured to download the pages linked to a site of interest, and the automated subject assignment and terminology extraction programs can be applied the entire set of pages. But a more thorough analysis comes only at the cost of a time lag that may sometimes be unacceptable to the user.

Design

The purpose of the present study is to obtain feedback to determine whether the WordSmith software can identify descriptive concepts, called *lexical phrases* in this paper, that are also syntactically correct and complete. We conveyed our goal to the study participants by asking them to consider whether the concepts were "natural-sounding" and "good subject descriptors" for the sites. We devised a Web-based survey that instructs participants to examine ten Web sites already represented by records in the CORC database and to evaluate ten concepts extracted from each site for their effectiveness as subject descriptors. Yes-or-no judgments were submitted to a standard HTML checkbox form and anonymously aggregated at an HTTP server site managed by OCLC. Some participants in the pilot study said they would have preferred to give a rating instead of a binary decision, but a binary decision enables us to define an informed cutoff point for selecting the best words and phrases in a ranked list of WordSmith output.

The concepts were extracted using all of the heuristics described in Section 3 that reasonably pertain to relatively short, isolated documents. The ranking heuristic was a function of the following factors:

- *Raw frequency.* Highly frequent words and phrases were ranked higher than low-frequency tokens. Since the output contains only noun phrases and is normalized to exclude numbers, dates and pronouns, words that normally appear at the top of a frequency tabulation of English text are excluded.

- *Frequency of the noun phrase heads.* Words or phrases containing high-ly frequent noun phrase heads were ranked higher. This would ensure that in an article about gene therapy, the word *gene* and the phrases *anti-cancer genes, gene treatment, gene therapy, tumor suppressor genes* and *anti-cancer genes* would be ranked high, even if the absolute frequency of any of the phrases turns out to be relatively low. A head is identified as the rightmost word in a noun phrase and is counted in whatever other contexts it appears, either as the isolated word *gene*, or as the modifier in *gene therapy* or *gene treatment*.
- *Position in the document.* There is a small but growing body of research in the computational linguistics literature on the relationship between discourse structure and the location of terminology that reveals the sub-ject of the document. In our heuristic, words or phrases appearing early in the document were ranked higher than those appearing near the end. Of course, this is the minimal amount of discourse structure that can be encoded, but it is generically useful, it eliminates the banners, buttons and copyright statements found at the bottom of many Web pages, and can be calculated quickly in the real-time applications that we envision.

The results of the ranking heuristic can be illustrated in a list of phrases obtained from a page in the Dublin Core Web site, which we used in prelimi-nary tests and will use for illustration because the concepts are probably familiar to the usual audience of the *Journal of Internet Cataloging*. The phrases in the left column of Table 3 are at the top of the list of the Word-Smith output and primarily show the effects of the noun-phrase-head ranking heuristic that hints at the topics receiving the most development in connected text. The phrases on the right are from the bottom of the list and show topics that are mentioned only incidentally or are found in references, footnotes, banners, or site navigation instructions.

Pilot tests showed that there was such high agreement about the status of the words and phrases at the bottom of the ranked list that they could be reasonably excluded from further study. Accordingly, the concepts selected

TABLE 3. Ranked WordSmith output from a Dublin Core Web document.

Dublin Core	decisions and discussions
Metadata	workshop series sponsors
resource description	meetings and results
resource	sitemap
content	glossary
publisher element description	repository
meta name	dienst
standardized descriptive metadata	service
metadata system	background reading

for evaluation in the present study are selected from the top two thirds of the list returned by the WordSmith ranking heuristic. Concepts randomly sampled from the first third of the list are proposed as good subject descriptors; those from the second third are poor. For each Web page to be evaluated, ten concepts are selected from these two rating categories and presented randomly to the judge. The evaluation study thus has a 2 x 2 factorial design that examines the rating source (WordSmith vs. human) and the type of rating (good vs. poor). The immediate purpose of the experiment is to determine whether the human rating agrees with the rating obtained from the Word-Smith ranking heuristic.

Results and Discussion

Table 4 shows the results obtained from 25 judges in the library community who participated in a study conducted at OCLC via a Web-based survey. The survey asked participants to rate the terminology extracted from ten Web sites, but only nine are included in our data analysis. On one site, a home page for news about Internet radio, judges supplied ratings for so few of the terms that we question whether the site was accessible throughout the two-week period of the test and whether its content remained stable.

Table 4 is a contingency table to which we have applied the Kappa measure, a statistic related to chi-square that measures agreement and is widely used in the computational linguistics community for tasks similar to ours. Kappa measures range from -1 (for perfect disagreement) to 1 (for perfect agreement). The consensus among computational linguists is that a satisfactory score for measuring the performance of software that categorizes objects against human judges is in the range of .6 to .8 (MUC-6 1995, Introduction). On our pilot data, we scored .57, which is very credible for our relatively small subject pool.

Table 4 reveals that there is high agreement about the poor terms. Among those terms ranked low by the WordSmith ranking algorithm, human judges

TABLE 4. WordSmith rankings and 25 CORC participants' ratings on terminology extracted from nine Web sites.

	High WS rank	Low WS rank	Totals
Judged good	819	177	996
Judged poor	306	948	1254
Totals	1125	1125	2250

Kappa = .57

rated most of them to be poor subject descriptors. This data suggests that even if we select only the first third of the terms in the ranked output, relatively few good terms are lost. But the judges also rated many of the terms ranked high by WordSmith to be poor descriptors, indicating that the WordSmith output can be made more useful by a more aggressive filter.

Table 5 shows sample terms from the four categories of ratings that correspond to the numeric values in Table 4. For illustration, Table 5 lists some concepts extracted from the Dublin Core Web Site that were used in a preliminary test.

The upper-left and lower-right quadrants represent successful matches between human judges and the WordSmith extraction and ranking software. As in Table 3, the effects of the heuristic that clusters noun phrases by their head terms are apparent. The two quadrants show the same range of syntactic forms, but the "poor" category shows more single nouns, while the "good" category has more noun-noun and adjective-noun phrases. The lower left and upper right quadrants illustrate WordSmith's current failures. In the upper right quadrant, which represents subject descriptors rated "good" by judges but ranked low by WordSmith, the words and phrases sometimes contained frequent noun-phrase heads, such as *element*, *description*, and *metadata*, but had a low absolute frequency and were outranked by phrases such as *purpose*

TABLE 5. Sample categorizations of WordSmith output.

	High WordSmith rank	Low WordSmith rank
Judged good	Metadata Metadata conversion Dublin Core Nordic DC Metadata Creator Dublin Core elements Dublin Core for museum information Collection management and resource discovery RDF-encoded Dublin Core	Automatic RDF metadata generator Resource discovery metadata ISO date profile Publisher element description Educational qualifiers RDF community Local elements Euler service
Judged poor	Purpose of Dublin Core Draft date General usefulness for Dublin Core applications Metadata standards in use Description Relation Mailing list discussions Dublin Core members Resource	Goal Textual studies Java Purpose Common user interface Collections of articles Usability Creation Changes without clear evidence

of Dublin Core and *general usefulness of Dublin Core applications*. These results suggest that not every noun phrase containing a frequent head is a valuable concept and that noun phrases containing prepositions and conjunctions must be weighted differently in an improved version of the WordSmith ranking heuristic.

The source material from the main study includes Web sites for Chinese medicine and women's health, the American Mathematical Society, Victor Borges, the MacMillan Law Library at the University of Georgia, and welding for instrument-making and machine tools. It is more difficult to make generalizations about the ratings of the terminology extracted from this diverse collection than from the single collection of Web sites about metadata used in the pilot study. But the highest ratings were overwhelmingly given to personal, geographic, and corporate names. Most names were also assigned high ranks by WordSmith, but occasionally they were not, accounting for some of the mismatches recorded in the upper right quadrant in Table 4. Among the terms ranked low by WordSmith and rated low by the human judges were many that identified topics with minor coverage on their respective Web pages, such as *Borges conferences* on the Borges site and *quality control* on the welding site, as well as many terms having to do with navigation and characteristics of the Web page, such as *guestbook* and *e-mail survey*.

One point of genuine confusion was the specificity of the term or phrase. Many sets of terminology for a given Web page included more and less specific terms, such as *Michigan* and *University of Michigan* or *welding* and *TIG welding*, and neither the WordSmith ranks or the judges' ratings were consistent.

OTHER USES OF AUTOMATICALLY EXTRACTED TERMINOLOGY

The study described in this paper is designed to simulate the task of automatically identifying the words and phrases in a Web page that might be added as uncontrolled subject terminology to a CORC record. But the task at hand has obvious limits because it can't be completely automated. Cataloging expertise is difficult to model and may vary according to local conventions. Moreover, the text of the Web sites that have attracted the attention of the library community so far often present what amounts to a worst-case test of the WordSmith software.

Nevertheless, the results from this study will improve the concept-extraction feature currently implemented in experimental versions of the CORC software and will help us evaluate WordSmith for other uses in the CORC project. For example, we are actively studying the relationship between

TABLE 6. Some current topics in the CORC database.

Digital age	Distance education
Digital archive	Distance education and communication
Digital archiving	Distance Education Association
Digital audio tape	Distance education classes
Digital camera(s)	Distance education conference(s)
Digital classics	Distance education course(s)
Digital collection(s)	Distance education graduate program(s)
Digital data	Distance education institutions
Digital database	Distance education Internet
Digital design team	Distance education materials
Digital Equipment Corporation	Distance education program(s)
Digital form	Distance education project(s)
Digital format	Distance education research
Digital image data	Distance education resources
Digital images	Distance education students
Digital imaging	Distance education track
Digital librarian	Distance learning and distance
Digital library	Distance learning and telemedicine
Digital library collections	Distance learning and telemedicine program
Digital library initiative	Distance Learning Centre of Victoria
Digital library projects	Distance learning network
Digital millennium	Distance learning programs
Digital photography	Distance learning projects
Digital printing	Distance learning resource center
Digital resources	Distance learning students
Digital scriptorium	Distance learning technologies
Digital signal	Distance learning technology
Digital signal processing	
Digital signal processing group	
Digital signature(s)	
Digital technologies	
Digital video	

WordSmith and automatic subject assignment using the Dewey Decimal Classification. As we argued in Vizine-Goetz and Godby (1997) and Godby and Reighart (1998), it is sometimes possible to map terminology found in collections of full-text documents to the Dewey Decimal Classification, making it more responsive in future classification tasks. This is a long-term goal, but the techniques described in this paper have a more immediate use. When automatic classification of a Web document is based only on the words and phrases ranked in the top third of the list returned by WordSmith, the results are more precise, reflecting the fact that classification is based only on the concepts that are the most pertinent to the subject of the document. Results of our experiments with this use of WordSmith should be visible within the next six months.

The WordSmith software can also produce indexes of the Web documents in the CORC database, creating another mode of subject access that complements the information found in CORC records. Table 6 shows part of an index obtained from the Web documents described in the CORC database as of June 1999 that is especially rich in novelty, specificity, and linguistic currency.

Such lists may be valuable in their current form. They could be made available as browsable subject indexes that contain many concepts not found in current editions of standard library subject classification schemes, or perhaps even as static terminology resources that aid the cataloger. We are also exploring ways to organize them with thesaurus-like relations such as *broader* and *narrower*. The WordSmith home page (WordSmith 1999) has pointers to research papers and demonstrations that develop these ideas.

REFERENCES

Mitchell, J., Editor. (1996). Dewey Decimal Classification and Relative Index, Edition 21. Forest Press. Albany, New York.

Pamela Downing (1977). On the creation and use of English compound nouns. *Language* 53:4, 810-842.

Dublin Core (1999). The Dublin Core Web Site. Accessible at: *http://purl.org/DC/documents/*.

Godby, C. (1999). Toward an organized base of terminology from Web documents. OCLC Newsletter. September/October.

Godby, C. and Reighart, R. (1998c). Using Machine-Readable Text as a Source of Novel Vocabulary to Update the Dewey Decimal Classification. Presented at the Association of Information Science Special Interest Group on Classification Research (ASIS-SIG/CR), October 25, 1998. Accessible at: *purl/oclc/wordsmith*.

Hickey, T. (1998). Cooperative Online Resource Catalog explores uses for catalog of Internet resources. OCLC Newsletter, September/October, No. 235. Accessible at: *http://www.oclc.org/oclc/new/n235/cooperative_online_resource_catalog.htm*.

Koch, T. (1998). Nutzung von Klassifikationssystemen zur verbesserten Beschreibung, Organization und Suche von Internet Ressourcen. Manuskript 15.3.98. Accessible at: *http://www.ub2.lu.se/tk/publ/bubmanus.html*.

Marchand, Hans (1969). *Categories and Types of Present-day English Word Formation*. Munich: C.H. Beck'sche Verlagsbuchhandllung.

MUC-6. (1995). Message Understanding Conference (MUC-6), Proceedings of a Conference Held in Columbia, Maryland, November 6-8, 1995. Proceedings distributed by Morgan Kaufmann Publishers, San Francisco, Ca.

Nakagawa, H. and Kori, T. (1998). Nested collocation and compound noun for term extraction. *Computerm '98: Proceedings from the First Workshop on Computational Terminology*. Montreal, Quebec, Canada: COLING-ACL. 64-70.

Vizine-Goetz, D. (2000). Dewey in CORC: classification in metadata and pathfinders. *Journal of Internet Cataloging*, 4(1/2), 67-80.

Vizine-Goetz, D. (1998a May/June). Subject headings for everyone: popular Library of Congress Subject Headings with Dewey numbers. *OCLC Newsletter*, 29-33.

Vizine-Goetz, D. 1998b. Dewey as an Internet Subject Guide. In Proceedings of the Fifth International ISKO Conference, Lille, 25-29 August 1998. Würzburg: Ergon Verlag. 191-97. Available at <*http://www.oclc.org/~vizine/isko/vizine-goetz_isko5.htm*>.

Vizine-Goetz, D. and Godby, C. (1996). Library classification schemes and access to electronic collections: enhancement of the Dewey Decimal Classification with supplemental vocabulary. *Advances in Classification Research Volume 7: Proceedings of the ASIS SIG/CR Classification Research Workshop*, Silver Spring, MD: American Society for Information Science.

Wacholder, N. (1998). Simplex NPs clustered by head: a method for identifying significant topics within a document. *The Computational Treatment of Nominals: Proceedings of the Workshop*. Montreal, Quebec, Canada: COLING-ACL. 70-79.

WordSmith. (1999). The WordSmith home page. Accessible at: *http://orc.rsch.oclc.org:5061/*.

Dewey in CORC:
Classification in Metadata
and Pathfinders

Diane Vizine-Goetz

SUMMARY. The Cooperative Online Resource Catalog project (CORC) is providing an opportunity for OCLC researchers and Dewey editors[1] to explore the potential of the Dewey Decimal Classification (DDC) system for organizing electronic resources. Efforts to enrich the content of the DDC database through vocabulary mapping projects have improved the ability of CORC users to employ classification in metadata records and pathfinders. Mapped vocabulary is used in the following ways: (1) to improve access to Dewey by expanding the indexing vocabulary; (2) to assist in the assignment of subject elements during metadata creation; (3) to provide supplemental terminology for automated classification; and (4) to provide alternative access mechanisms or views to resources in the CORC database. *[Article copies available for a fee from The Haworth Document Delivery Service: 1-800-342-9678. E-mail address: <getinfo@haworthpressinc.com> Website: <http://www.HaworthPress.com>]*

KEYWORDS. DDC, Dewey Decimal Classification, LCSH, Library of Congress Subject Headings, vocabulary mapping

VOCABULARY MAPPING PROJECTS

In 1994, OCLC staff began enhancing the vocabulary of the DDC by mapping Library of Congress Subject Headings (LCSH) to the Dewey

---

Diane Vizine-Goetz is a Research Scientist in the OCLC Office of Research (e-mail: vizine@oclc.org).

[Haworth co-indexing entry note]: "Dewey in CORC: Classification in Metadata and Pathfinders." Vizine-Goetz, Diane. Co-published simultaneously in *Journal of Internet Cataloging* (The Haworth Information Press, an imprint of The Haworth Press, Inc.) Vol. 4, No. 1/2, 2001, pp. 67-80; and: *CORC: New Tools and Possibilities for Cooperative Electronic Resource Description* (ed: Karen Calhoun, and John J. Riemer) The Haworth Information Press, an imprint of The Haworth Press, Inc., 2001, pp. 67-80. Single or multiple copies of this article are available for a fee from The Haworth Document Delivery Service [1-800-342-9678, 9:00 a.m. - 5:00 p.m. (EST). E-mail address: getinfo@haworthpressinc.com].

scheme. In this initial effort, LC subject headings were statistically mapped to DDC classes and included in the Electronic Dewey CD-ROM database. Although the Dewey editors have always used LC subject headings as a source for terminology in the DDC Relative Index, at the end of 1995, they began to add intellectually mapped LCSH to a separate index in the Dewey editorial database (Mitchell, 1996). These two efforts laid the groundwork for a series of mapping projects to extend the vocabulary base in the DDC. Our recent work has focused on intellectual or statistical mappings of LC subject headings from the following sources:

- LCSH Weekly lists[2]
- LCSH and LC children's headings assigned to juvenile materials
- LCSH assigned to OCLC NetFirst records
- Statistically mapped LCSH from WorldCat

Mappings of other subject heading lists and thesauri to DDC are planned or underway (e.g., MeSH, A Women's Thesaurus).[3]

Enhancing the DDC vocabulary with other subject vocabularies expands the knowledge base and improves access to Dewey itself as well as to DDC-organized collections. For many years, Marcia Bates has advocated the development of user-friendly access mechanisms that incorporate multiple terms of access for a given concept (1986, 1998). The Dewey vocabulary mapping projects are a step in this direction.

Statistical Mappings

Statistically mapped terms from the WorldCat database provide access to the actual LCSH/DDC associations used in bibliographic data and often show relationships among LC subject headings not provided for through the LCSH cross reference structure. For example, the headings **Bird attracting**, **Bird watching**, and **Birding sites** are linked to the concept **Bird watching** (598.07234) in Dewey, though none are linked together by the LCSH cross-reference structure. Statistically mapped headings also show DDC associations for headings that are authorized by the rules for LC heading construction, but not represented in the subject heading list or authority file. An example is the heading **Birds–Feeding and Feeds**, in Table 1. Statistical mappings also provide access to name subject headings that have been associated with a given Dewey concept, e.g., see the entry **Golfers** (796.352092), in Table 1.

Editorial Mappings

Editorial mappings provide similar kinds of associations but can be focused in particular topic areas because they do not depend on usage thresh-

TABLE 1. DDC Classes and Mapped LCSH Vocabulary.

006.5 (Computer sound synthesis)		
Internet radio broadcasting	MP3 Players	
598.07234 (Bird watching)		
Bird attracting Birds—Feeding and feeds	Bird watching	Birding sites
796.352092 (Golfers)		
Hogan, Ben, 1912-	Jones, Bobby, 1902-1971	Nelson, Byron, 1912-
Nicklaus, Jack Trevino, Lee	Norman, Greg, 1955- Woods, Tiger	Palmer, Arnold, 1929- Zaharias, Babe Didrikson, 1911-1956

olds to form relevant associations. For instance, a project was undertaken to link LC headings for Native Americans to DDC. Another provided LCSH associations in an area of Dewey that had been extensively revised. Editorial mapping of subject vocabulary serves another important function. It provides a mechanism for rapidly linking new topics to Dewey. The heading, **MP3 players**, from Weekly List number 46,[4] is a good example of a new LCSH recently linked to Dewey. Although this topic is not new to the Web (it receives more than 13,000 hits on AltaVista), it is relatively new to more traditional library databases (retrieving only 2 records in WorldCat during the same time).[5]

As the last example illustrates, a major disadvantage of both approaches is that they are essentially reactive, since they depend on pre-established terminology as the source vocabulary. In order to address emerging topics, research into proactive processes is needed. At OCLC, Godby and Reighart are using computational linguistics techniques to explore concept identification, and mapping takes place before a concept appears in a subject heading list or thesaurus (1998, 2000).

THE ENHANCED DDC DATABASE

Term associations are merged with selected data from the DDC 21 editorial database to form the enhanced DDC database. The editorial database is an up-to-date version of the classification that contains all of the information needed to maintain and print the DDC. The enhanced database also contains revisions of DDC captions at the top-most levels of Dewey. The enhanced DDC database is the version of the DDC used in CORC.

The Dewey database in CORC is searchable by Dewey numbers and by words from DDC captions, notes, Relative Index terms, and mapped LCSH vocabulary. The database can also be browsed by Relative Index term, LC Subject Heading, and a Keywords in Context (for Relative Index terms and mapped LCSH vocabulary). A typical record display, shown in Figure 1, includes the Dewey class number, caption, hierarchy, notes, and terminology

FIGURE 1. Dewey Record in CORC for class number 004.678 (Internet).

Dewey Class:	004.678
Class Caption:	Internet
0x	Main Topics
0xx	Computers, Information & General Reference
00x	Computers, Internet & Systems
004	Data processing Computer science
004.6	Interfacing and communications
004.65-004.68	Computer communications networks
004.67	Wide-area networks
004.678	**Internet**

Notes

Class a specific regional or national network with the area served, e.g., Janet 004.6780941

* Use notation T1--019 from Table 1 as modified at 004.019

See Manual at 004.678 vs. 025.04, 384.33

Dewey Index Terms	LC Subject Headings	IM	SHC	NF	SM	FM
Internet	HTTP (Computer network protocol)	+				
	Internet (Computer network)				+	+
	Internet (Computer network)--Handbooks, manuals, etc					+
	Internet addresses	+				
	Internet consultants	+		+		
	Internet domain names	+				
	Internet service providers	+				
	WebTV (Trademark)					+
	World Wide Web (Information retrieval system)				+	+

(Relative Index terms and mapped LCSH vocabulary). In this example, revised caption headings are visible in the Dewey hierarchy. The heading **Computers, Information and General Reference** has replaced the former heading, **Generalities**, at the first level (represented as 0xx in the CORC Dewey display).

Mapped subject terms are displayed in a table in the lower portion of the Dewey record. The column heading labels are linked to a description of the source of the term and the method used to associate the subject heading with the class number (see Table 2). The strength of the association varies depending upon the mapping method (intellectual or statistical) and source. A plus sign (+) is placed in the column for a term from a given source (see Figure 1). Terms may be mapped from multiple sources.

Terms with the IM designation have the strongest association–Dewey editorial staff members have intellectually mapped them to the DDC. Terms with an SHC designation are also strongly associated with the DDC, but often at a broader Dewey number that represents the concept in the abridged edition of DDC.[6] Terms designated as NF have been linked to DDC by OCLC NetFirst editors. The two remaining sets of terms have been automatically linked to the DDC using statistical techniques. The abbreviation SM is used to identify terms associated with the DDC using a term co-occurrence measure. This measure was applied to more than 710,000 WorldCat records that contain MARC 082 (Dewey Decimal Classification number) and LC Subject Heading fields, MARC tag 600-651. (See Vizine-Goetz, 1999, for a more detailed discussion on the application of this measure.) The terms labeled FM consist of LC subject headings from WorldCat that are included in the Dewey for Windows database and that have been mapped to DDC using a simpler statistical technique. About 90,000 LCSH mappings are contained in the enhanced DDC database.

TABLE 2. Source and association method for mapped vocabulary in CORC.

CORC Abbreviation	Source of Term	Association Method	Strength of Relationship
IM	Editorially mapped LCSH	Intellectual	Strong
SHC	Subject Headings for Children	Intellectual	Strong
NF	LCSH assigned in Netfirst records	Intellectual	Moderate
SM	OCLC WorldCat	Statistical	Moderate to Strong
FM	Dewey for Windows (from WorldCat)	Statistical	Moderate to Weak

CLASSIFICATION IN METADATA

Manual Classifying

The CORC tool set includes several facilities for applying DDC numbers in CORC metadata records. At the most basic level of functionality, Dewey numbers can be directly input in either the MARC or Dublin Core views. Authority control can then be applied for numbers contained in the enhanced DDC 21 database. When a number is authority controlled, a link is formed from the number in the metadata record to the Dewey record in the CORC Dewey database. The DDC caption is also inserted into the metadata record. An example of a CORC metadata record with authority controlled DDC numbers is shown in Figure 2.

The DDC number link in any of the controlled Dewey number fields leads to the display of the corresponding Dewey record, e.g., clicking on 004.678

FIGURE 2. Dublin Core record with DDC numbers.

CORC:	213436	Created:	OCL	2000-01-13	
Status:	Complete	Modified:	OCL	2000-02-15	
Title	OCLC/Forest Press/news/new on this web site				
Description	Title from title screen.				
Description.Summary	Provides links to new items on OCLC Forest Press Web site.				
Creator.CorporateName	Forest Press.				
Date.Issued	2000-01-13				
Format.MIME	text/html; charset=8859-1				
Identifier.URL	http://www.oclc.org/oclc/fp/news/newweb.htm				
Language	English				
Publisher	[OCLC Online Computer Library Center, Inc.]				
Publisher.Place	[Dublin, Ohio] :				
Relation.Requires	Mode of access: World Wide Web.				
Subject.DDC Local	004.678	Internet			
Subject.DDC Local	025.431	Dewey Decimal Classification			
Subject.LCSH	World Wide Web.				
Subject.CorporateName	Forest Press.				
Subject.LCSH	Classification, Dewey decimal.				
Subject.DDC-Scorpion	025.4	Subject analysis and control			

causes the system to display DDC record for 004.678 (see Figure 1). All elements of the hierarchy are links, making it easy to navigate to broader or narrower classes. The hierarchy display itself is important because it gives the context for a given Dewey class. Navigation from one Dewey record to another is further facilitated by Dewey number links in the notes fields of the DDC records. For Dewey record 004.678 (**Internet**), the link *T1–019* leads to the display of the Table 1 record for 019, the link 004.019 to the corresponding schedule record, and the link 004.678 vs. 025.04, 384.33 to the appropriate record from the Dewey manual.

Many of the mapped LC subject headings in the terminology portion of the record are themselves links, in this case, into the LCSH authority file available in CORC. The LCSH terms associated with Dewey records serve many functions in CORC. First, mapped terminology improves access to Dewey by expanding the indexing vocabulary. In CORC, Dewey record 004.678 is retrievable by its caption and Relative Index term, **Internet**, but also by the mapped vocabulary that includes such terms as, *HTTP*, *computer network*, *Internet domain names*, *Internet service providers*, and *World Wide Web*.

Second, mapped headings have the potential to assist in the assignment of subject elements during metadata creation. The enhanced DDC records bring together many headings that would be more difficult to locate through the subject heading system alone. For instance, **HTTP (Computer network protocol)** and **World Wide Web (Information retrieval system)**, or **Internet addresses** and **Internet domain names**, or **Bird watching** and **Birding sites**. These examples demonstrate the power of an improved classification knowledge base linked with a separate subject vocabulary to show novel and implied relationships among complementary subject schemes. Currently, users need to 'copy and paste' the LC subject headings from the Dewey records into their CORC metadata description, but in the future it may be possible to provide a method to easily add LCSH links to metadata records from within the DDC displays. Some CORC users, who otherwise are uninterested in applying DDC numbers, may find this feature attractive.

(Semi) Automatic Classification

A third use of the mapped vocabulary is to provide supplemental terminology for the automated classification database. A program called Scorpion, developed by OCLC, is used to do the automatic class number assignment. The DDC data files used to perform the automated classification contain mapped vocabulary from the enhanced DDC database.

In CORC, a user can create a metadata record by having the system generate a preliminary record from a Web-accessible resource. The system will also attempt to automatically assign DDC numbers if the 'Generate Dewey numbers' option is used. When the option is used, the software

FIGURE 3a

locates the resource, extracts information, performs the automatic classification using the extracted data and inserts the numbers into the CORC metadata record in a field named Subject.DDC-Scorpion. During the automated classification process, a set of terms is extracted from the resource being cataloged and used to retrieve a ranked list of DDC numbers from the terminology-enhanced database. The ranking is based on relative frequency of occurrence of terms and other criteria relating to associations found in the Dewey classification. The highest ranking class numbers are inserted into the preliminary record and displayed to the creator of the metadata description. The preliminary record, including the automatically generated class, can then be revised or enhanced by the user.

Automatic classification is an area of active research at OCLC. There are several projects underway to improve the accuracy of the automated classification routines. One of these is investigating the use of more sophisticated word extraction routines that identify key phrases within documents (Godby and Reighart, 2000). The current system often suggests several class numbers

FIGURE 3b

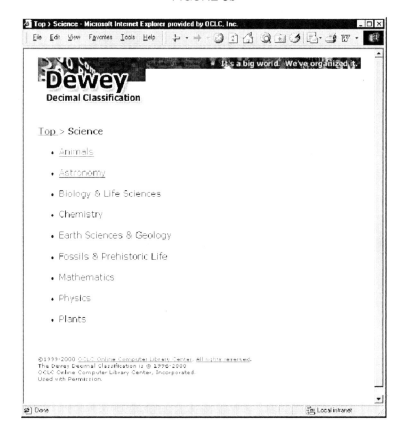

that are either exact or very close (see Scorpion-class number in Figure 2) to the proper numbers. However, human review of the numbers is still needed because, on occasion, the suggested class numbers are far from the mark.

Alternative Views Through the DDC

The renamed Dewey captions at the top two levels in CORC present an alternative way for accessing the DDC. Specialized captions that were intended exclusively for classifiers have been mapped to captions that are more current and expressive. Dewey has other features that make it a useful access mechanism for browsing and retrieval. The well-developed hierarchies in Dewey provide a method of moving around (the knowledge structure) that is easily grasped and used. The decimal notation aids in revealing the hierarchy, and class numbers in Dewey have the same meaning across languages. As

FIGURE 3c

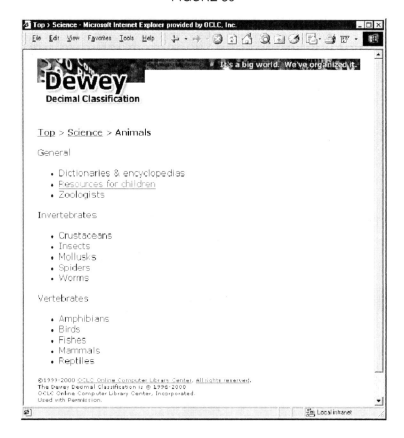

non-English language versions of the DDC captions become more available, it will be possible to provide views of the DDC in CORC (or to CORC metadata records classified by Dewey) based upon user language preferences. For instance, the caption for DDC number 551.65 could be displayed as follows for English language users, French language users, and Spanish language users, respectively:

- Weather forecasts and reports for specific areas
- Prévisions et bulletins météorologiques pour des régions déterminées
- Pronósticos e informes del tiempo atmosférico para áreas específicas

These alternative views could be generated based on other user preferences, such as age or grade level, subject specialty, familiarity with Dewey, etc. OCLC researchers are exploring this idea by constructing a series of experimental CORC pathfinders accessible from a restructured set of DDC classes (see Figure 3a). This presentation of the DDC diverges from traditional 10s-based representations. Levels have been split or combined into fewer or more groups as needed. There really is no limit on how the structure can be displayed as long as the meaning, scope, and relationship among classes is retained. In Figure 3b, the presentation of topics for Science follows Dewey much more closely than the top level–all of the sub-disciplines of Science (500) are represented, although in alphabetical order rather than by DDC number. At the next level, under the label General (Figure 3c), non-topical or non-primary aspects of the subject are provided by presenting topics that correspond to class numbers built by adding notation from Dewey Table 1 (Standard subdivisions). The lowest level (Figure 3d) is a departure from

FIGURE 3d

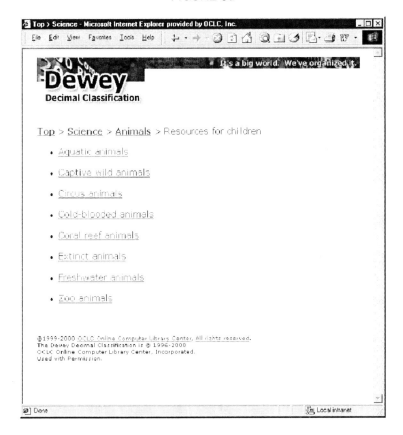

topics directly represented in Dewey, but instead is a presentation of LCSH vocabulary mapped to Dewey. In this case, selected headings from *Subject Headings for Children* (1998) are displayed. These headings have been editorially mapped to DDC classes for animals. The DDC pathfinders that are accessible through the experimental DDC Web browser are constructed entirely by executing searches against the CORC database for records containing Dewey numbers, mapped terminology, or both. (Figure 4). This last example illustrates how the enhanced DDC database, enriched with mapped vocabulary, is being used to provide an alternative access mechanism or view for electronic resources in the CORC catalog database. For more information on how Dewey can be used to provide alternative views, see Mitchell (1998).

FIGURE 4

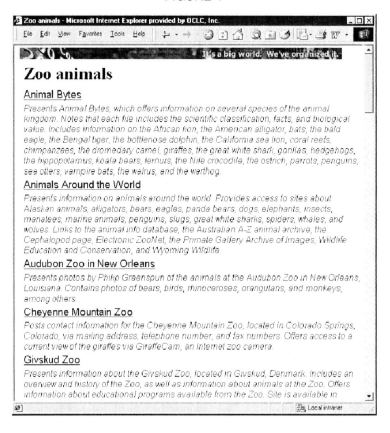

CONCLUSIONS

Deploying the DDC in the CORC system demonstrates how classification can be used in metadata. More importantly, Dewey into CORC represents the next generation of knowledge engineering tools for Web resources. This implementation exploits the rich knowledge structure of the DDC, i.e., its well-defined categories, well-developed hierarchies and extensive network of relationships, while providing access to an improved classification database that has been linked with complementary subject vocabularies. A knowledge structure such as this, which is capable of showing new and indirect relationships among subjects, will be needed for organizing diverse collections that include both traditional and electronic resources.

NOTES

1. OCLC research staff members: Carol Hickey, Andrew Houghton, Roger Thompson, and Diane Vizine-Goetz. Dewey editorial staff members: Julianne Beall, Giles Martin, Winton Matthews, Joan Mitchell, and Gregory New.
2. Library of Congress Subject Headings Weekly Lists. Accessible at: http://lcweb.loc.gov/catdir/cpso/cpso.html#subjects
3. Hope Olsen and Denis Ward are experimenting with mapping A Women's Thesaurus to the DDC to overlay the relationships found in women's studies on the existing Dewey structure (Olson and Ward, 1998). See also, Finding Spaces for Feminism in Traditional Library Classification: Dewey Decimal Classification, Windows and the World Wide Web, Accessible at: http://www.ualberta.ca/~holson/femddc/
4. Library of Congress Subject Headings Weekly Lists 46 (November 17, 1999). Accessible at http://lcweb.loc.gov/catdir/cpso/wls99/awls9946.html
5. February 14, 2000.
6. These LC subject headings were extracted from the WorldCat database by processing LC MARC records with headings used in the LC Annotated Card Program (AC)/Subject Headings for Children's Literature, then the candidate mappings were reviewed by the Dewey editors to match numbers in Abridged Edition 13.

REFERENCES

Bates, Marcia J. 1986. Subject access in online catalogs: A design model. *Journal of the American Society for Information Science* 37 (1986): 357-376.
Bates, Marcia J. 1998. Indexing and access for digital libraries and the Internet: human, database, and domain factors. *Journal of the American Society for Information Science* 49 (1998): 1185-1205. Manuscript accessible at: http://dlis.gseis.ucla.edu/research/mjbates.html
Godby, Carol J., and Reighart, Ray. 1998. Using machine-readable text as a source of novel vocabulary to update the Dewey Decimal Classification. Paper presented at

the 9th ASIS SIG/CR Classification Research Workshop, October 25, 1998. Also available at: http://orc.rsch.oclc.org:5061/papers/sigcr98.html

Godby, Carol J., and Reighart, Ray. Terminology identification in a collection of Web resources. *Journal of Internet Cataloging* 4(1/2) (2001): 49-65.

Mitchell, Joan. S. 1996. The Dewey Decimal Classification at 120: Edition 21 and beyond. In *Knowledge organization and change: Proceedings of the 4th international ISKO conference*, ed. R. Green, 378-385. Frankfurt/Main: INDEKS Verlag.

Mitchell, Joan S. 1998. Flexible structures in the Dewey Decimal Classification. *Knowledge Organization* 25 (1998): 156-158.

Olson, Hope A., and Ward, Dennis. B. Charting a journey across knowledge domains: Feminism in the Dewey Decimal Classification. In *Structure and relations in knowledge organization: Proceedings of the 5th international ISKO conference*, ed. W. Mustafa el-Hadi, J. Maniez, & A.S. Pollitt, 238-244. Würzburg: Ergon Verlag, 1998.

Vizine-Goetz, Diane. 1998. Subject headings for everyone: Popular Library of Congress Subject Headings with Dewey numbers. *OCLC Newsletter* May/June 1998 No. 233. Available at: http://www.oclc.org/oclc/new/n233/rsch_subj_headings_ everyone.htm.

Winkel, Lois. 1998. *Subject headings for children: a list of subject headings used by the Library of Congress with abridged Dewey numbers added.* Dublin, OH: Forest Press.

Crosswalking Metadata
in the OCLC CORC Service

Eric Childress

SUMMARY. The new OCLC CORC service will offer users the ability to create, edit, or export metadata in several standard views, chiefly MARC and Dublin Core. This is made possible by a crosswalk, a specification for converting metadata from one standard to another. The article describes the philosophy and approach guiding the OCLC CORC service's implementation of its crosswalk capabilities. *[Article copies available for a fee from The Haworth Document Delivery Service: 1-800-342-9678. E-mail address: <getinfo@haworthpressinc.com> Website: <http://www.HaworthPress. com>]*

KEYWORDS. OCLC Online Computer Library Center, Inc., OCLC CORC service, crosswalks, metadata, MARC, Dublin Core

INTRODUCTION

OCLC Online Computer Library Center, Inc. is introducing a new group of tools and databases, the OCLC CORC service.[1] Designed to improve the

---

Eric Childress is Senior Product Support Specialist, OCLC Online Computer Library Center, Inc. (e-mail: eric_childress@oclc.org).

At this writing (February 2000), the finer points of design and implementation for OCLC Online Computer Library Center, Inc.'s July 2000 release of the OCLC CORC service are still in process. Accordingly, this description of its capabilities is less detailed than would suit a full discussion of the system's metadata format conversion capabilities.

[Haworth co-indexing entry note]: "Crosswalking Metadata in the OCLC CORC Service." Childress, Eric. Co-published simultaneously in *Journal of Internet Cataloging* (The Haworth Information Press, an imprint of The Haworth Press, Inc.) Vol. 4, No. 1/2, 2001, pp. 81-88; and: *CORC: New Tools and Possibilities for Cooperative Electronic Resource Description* (ed: Karen Calhoun, and John J. Riemer) The Haworth Information Press, an imprint of The Haworth Press, Inc., 2001, pp. 81-88. Single or multiple copies of this article are available for a fee from The Haworth Document Delivery Service [1-800-342-9678, 9:00 a.m. - 5:00 p.m. (EST). E-mail address: getinfo@haworthpressinc.com].

cooperative creation and maintenance of metadata (i.e., data about data or in this case, *structured* data about data) for networked information resources, the OCLC CORC service will also serve as a new platform for broadening the range of metadata formats that OCLC supports.

On its initial release, the OCLC CORC service will offer support for the Dublin Core Metadata Element Set (hereafter referred to as the Dublin Core)[2] and OCLC-MARC (MAchine Readable Cataloging)[3] as available views of all *resource records* ("resource records" are equivalent in scope, if not necessarily in format, to "bibliographic records") contained in the OCLC CORC Resource Catalog. The OCLC CORC service will allow users to create, edit, and display resource records in several variations of these two views and offer support for export of resource records in a user's choice of OCLC-MARC, Dublin Core HTML, or Dublin Core Resource Description Framework (RDF) Extensible Markup Language (XML).

The key to supporting multiple metadata "views" of the same resource record is a "crosswalk," which St. Pierre and LaPlant define as "a specification for mapping one metadata standard to another."[4] In other words, a crosswalk is a metadata-to-metadata conversion specification. Crosswalks may be the basis for human hand-conversion of metadata or implemented as a set of rules into machine processes.

The number and variety of crosswalks that have been created is modest but growing,[5] no doubt in response to the need for better interoperability (i.e., reusability) of metadata in an age of proliferating in-use and proposed metadata standards. It should be noted that there is criticism in some quarters of the development and use of crosswalks–many would prefer the effort expended on crosswalks to be spent, instead, on promoting the use of "universal" metadata standards. Even if someday a universally accepted metadata standard gains wide following, the development and maintenance of crosswalks seems likely to remain a necessary and ongoing activity for the conversion of legacy data. Interestingly, the Dublin Core–probably the leading candidate for a "universal" standard–is being purposefully designed to serve as both a metadata standard and the common convert-to/from metadata standard of crosswalks (i.e., metadata captured in two specialized formats could be converted via the Dublin Core as a common intermediate format).

OTHER METADATA CONVERSION ACTIVITY

As the world's largest library cooperative, OCLC is no stranger to building sophisticated metadata conversion utilities. Currently, OCLC is able to convert a number of major national MARC bibliographic formats and even some non-MARC formats (e.g., SGML files)–converting data in most cases to OCLC-MARC format. Additionally, OCLC has developed an excellent

OCLC-MARC-to/from-UNIMARC capability that supports online and off-line output of UNIMARC records from OCLC's WorldCat (the OCLC Online Union Catalog).

Although the initial version of the OCLC CORC service will provide editing, display, and crosswalk support for the Dublin Core and OCLC-MARC only, OCLC plans to develop additional capabilities for other major metadata standards in the future. Among the additional standards most highly requested by participants in the OCLC CORC research project has been support for the Text Encoding Initiative (TEI) header,[6] GEM Element Set,[7] Encoded Archival Description (EAD),[8] Content Standard for Digital Geospatial Metadata (CSDGM) (formerly known as the FGDC Metadata Standard),[9] and the VRA Core Categories.[10]

Conversion between similar metadata formats can be challenging, but conversion between unlike formats is often orders of magnitude more difficult. Though librarians have been influential in the evolution of the Dublin Core standard, there are very significant differences in approach between the Dublin Core and library standards such as the *International Bibliographic Description Standards* (and in the English-speaking community, our interpretation of ISBD, the *Anglo-American Cataloguing Rules*, 2nd edition, [AACR2]). These differences are inherent in and exacerbated by qualities of the library world's various flavors of MARC, the most favored standard inter-library metadata communications protocol. Heery,[11] Mandel,[12] Hopkins,[13] Gorman,[14] Caplan and Guenther,[15] among others, have articulated key points of convergence and conflicts that emerge in environments attempting to use and reconcile both the Dublin Core and MARC 21/AACR2. The evolution of library cataloging practice and adaptation of existing standards– or the establishment/adoption of new standards and practice–to more effectively address the special qualities of networked resources will ultimately drive resolution of some conflicts between emerging standards and established ones.

CORC'S CROSSWALK

While an element-by-element, field-by-field review of the OCLC CORC service's crosswalk no doubt merits discussion in a venue such as this article, the evolving state of the OCLC CORC service and the Dublin Core at this writing necessitates deferring such a detailed approach to a later date. With apologies to the reader, in substitution for such a detailed discussion, general principles guiding the development of the OCLC CORC service's crosswalk will be offered instead.

General principles guiding OCLC CORC service's crosswalk:

1. Embrace and, if necessary, extend industry standards
2. Emphasize the predictable and pragmatic
3. Engineer for robust performance and ease of enhancement
4. Expose as much as information content as practical in all supported views

1. Embrace and, if necessary, extend industry standards. OCLC is committed to adopting and promoting standards compliance and evolution.[16] Of particular application, in the context of the initial release of the OCLC CORC service, is the system's support of a Dublin Core-MARC crosswalk. The crosswalk of record is the Dublin Core/MARC/GILS Crosswalk published by the Library of Congress Network Development and MARC Standards Office.[17] OCLC has been collaborating closely with the Library of Congress in implementing OCLC CORC service's crosswalk based on this published specification. During its prototype stage, the OCLC CORC service has proven to be a useful test implementation of mapping in the Dublin Core/MARC/. GILS Crosswalk, and OCLC's experience has informed the revision and re-publication of the specification. Ongoing refinement of the OCLC CORC service's crosswalk capabilities (for Dublin Core-MARC plus additional standards over time) will continue to rely, whenever possible, on this caliber of world class expertise and published specifications. Additionally, OCLC will continue to contribute to the ongoing refinement of major standards and recommend improved harmonization whenever appropriate to facilitate global metadata exchange and expanded cooperation across libraries and with other communities.

2. Emphasize the predictable and pragmatic. While some loss of precision or content is inevitable in metadata conversion, particularly if conversions are frequently repeated for a given resource record, OCLC will emphasize consistent, predictable conversion behavior in the operation of OCLC CORC service's crosswalk–this may in some cases necessitate a pragmatic approach in the crosswalking of Dublin Core elements/qualifiers and MARC tags rather than theoretical precision in the reassignment of crosswalked data in Dublin Core elements/qualifiers or MARC tags and subfields. Participants in the OCLC CORC research project have emphasized the need for the system to support high productivity and effective and predictable, if not absolutely perfect, metadata mappings. The publication of library-oriented qualifiers for Dublin Core should minimize the loss of precision during crosswalking between library qualified Dublin Core and MARC 21/OCLC-MARC. Crosswalking data from any MARC format to unqualified Dublin Core will almost always result in precision loss because the Dublin Core Metadata Element set is a significantly simpler metadata format. The reverse, Dublin Core to MARC, if done well, will result in valid MARC, but in some cases less than perfect precision in assigning MARC tags and subfields.

3. Engineer for robust performance and ease of enhancement. Users will require rapid system responses to their requests for standard view changes so OCLC's implementation of OCLC CORC service crosswalks must balance sophistication with system performance. To assure that the crosswalk logic may be updated and adjusted easily and quickly as the underlying standards change or policy decisions are modified, OCLC CORC service developers have implemented special table-driven code creation routines. With the OCLC CORC service, OCLC is adopting a rapid development para-digm–system changes and upgrades will be installed on a more frequent basis than has been typical of most OCLC products.

4. Expose as much as information content as practical in all supported views. Based on the stated wishes of OCLC libraries participating in the OCLC CORC research project, OCLC will closely integrate OCLC CORC's Resource Catalog with WorldCat (the OCLC Online Union Catalog) so that resource records for networked resources originating in either database can be rapidly accessed by users of either system.[18] MARC's specificity is significantly higher than Dublin Core's, so library metadata-oriented qualifiers and extensions to Dublin Core will be developed and implemented in OCLC CORC service to enrich the Dublin Core view of OCLC-MARC-formatted metadata. For some data, formatting will be different in the respective views in order to accommodate different encoding schemes favored by each standard.

In addition to the crosswalk employed for real-time, interactive mode conversions of metadata, the OCLC CORC service has also been a locus for other metadata conversion activity:

- *Batchloading externally-generated metadata.* During the OCLC CORC research project, metadata in several non-MARC formats has been the subject of special efforts to create/adapt intellectual mapping and custom coding to prepare the data for loading into the CORC Resource Catalog. These efforts have required close consultation with the originating agency even when agencies have supplied "specification-compliant" files–non-MARC sources encountered so far have proven to be subject to varied interpretations even when based on common, published specifications. Conversion of non-MARC files to SGML (Standard Generalized Markup Language) format and then to OCLC-MARC has been the typical tactic, and this has generally been successful for converting a number of formats including GEM (Gateway for Educational Materials) records, TEI header databases, and others (including some home-grown formats). Decisions on how to mainstream this aspect of the OCLC CORC research project into OCLC's production batchloading routines are in process, but we're anticipating that lessons learned and code developed during the research phase will become part of an expanded repertory of conversion tools available for OCLC to use.

- *Automapping meta-tagged HTML.* During user-initiated harvesting of Web sites for building resource records in the OCLC CORC service, the system employs a sophisticated crosswalk (called an "automap") to convert harvested data into resource records. The OCLC CORC service's automapping routines for harvester data have been subject to fine-tuning and will likely require ongoing optimization for the foreseeable future–metadata, if available, in HTML resources is quite varied in its expression. OCLC is also investigating and, hopefully, will be able to support a greater range of object types (e.g., PDF) for harvesting.

- *Validation and record export.* Although mapping exists more in the background than foreground for validation and export functions, nevertheless, the OCLC CORC service applies rules and, in essence, a comparative map to pass or fail records based on their level of well-formedness. For OCLC-MARC validation, routines in use by the OCLC Cataloging System will be used, and a specification for validation of Dublin Core is being developed. Additionally, although not displayed in editable views/formats, on request, the OCLC CORC service will perform mapping/conversion of resource records to HTML Dublin Core meta-tags or Dublin Core RDF XML to allow users to preview resource records in these formats before exporting.

- *Administrative core.* Although not a category of information that has enjoyed the level of interest and effort as that garnered for metadata about resource objects, there is very practical need for exported Dublin Core resource records–such as MARC–to carry "administrative metadata"[19] or information-about-this-record data so that the metadata in HTML and XML can be extracted, stored, transmitted, and effectively manipulated as records in databases. OCLC will develop specifications for an administrative core and implement its administrative core in the OCLC CORC service's HTML and XML export options. The development and use of an administrative core in the DC HTML and DC RDF-XML outputs will lead to the OCLC CORC service's development of a crosswalk for selected MARC fields in support of the use of this administrative data add-on.

- *Vernacular characters.* The OCLC CORC service will support the Unicode character set and provide for conversion to/from the standard the ALA Character Set supported in OCLC Cataloging System so that users may export valid OCLC-MARC. Support for East Asian Character Code (EACC) and policies for addressing Unicode characters which cannot be converted to the ALA Character Set and/or EACC are still being developed at this writing. Some vernacular character features planned for the OCLC CORC service will not be available in the initial version of the service slated for release in mid-2000.

CONCLUSION

In summary, the OCLC CORC service represents a significant step forward in improving OCLC's support for the creation of metadata for networked resources. Among the system's capabilities will be support for an expanding array of metadata formats (initially limited to Dublin Core and OCLC-MARC), support for the Unicode Worldwide Character Standard,[20] and the implementation of sophisticated crosswalk capabilities that will allow individual resource records to be created, edited, displayed, and exported in a range of standard views/formats. The challenges of intellectual mapping and system engineering to assure consistent, robust, effective performance are significant, but OCLC will rely on the best specifications available, extend and refine these as necessary or develop new ones as needed, and engage in continuous improvement to the OCLC CORC service.

NOTES

1. "CORC" stands for Cooperative Online Resource Catalog.

2. For more information, see the official Dublin Core Metadata Initiative Web site: *http://purl.org/dc*

3. OCLC-MARC is based on *MARC 21 Format for Bibliographic Data* (Washington: Library of Congress, Cataloging Distribution Service, 1999-), a standard jointly maintained by the Library of Congress and the National Library of Canada. MARC 21 is widely used in the United States, Canada, and Australia.

4. St. Pierre, Margaret, and William P. LaPlant, Jr. "Issues in Crosswalking Content Metadata Standards" (Bethesda, Md.: National Information Standards Organization (NISO), Oct. 15, 1998): *http://www.niso.org/crsswalk.html*

5. A useful list of crosswalks likely to be of interest to the library community is maintained by Michael Day of UKOLN. See "Metadata: Mapping between Metadata Formats": *http://www.ukoln.ac.uk/metadata/interoperability/*

6. Text Encoding Initiative: *http://www.uic.edu/orgs/tei/*

7. Gateway for Educational Materials, see: *http://geminfo.org/Workbench/Metadata/ GEM_Element_List.html*

8. Encoded Archival Description: *http://www.loc.gov/ead/*

9. Content Standard for Digital Geospatial Metadata: *http://www.fgdc.gov/metadata/ contstan.html*

10. VRA Core Categories (published by the Visual Resource Association): *http://www.oberlin.edu/~art/vra/wc1.html*

11. Heery, Rachel. "Review of Metadata Formats," *Program*, vol. 30, no. 4, October 1996, pp. 355-362.

12. Mandel, Carol. "Manifestations of Cataloging in the Era of Metadata," ALCTS/LITA Institute on Managing Metadata for the Digital Library, May 4-5, 1998. *http://www.columbia.edu/cu/libraries/inside/projects/metadata/presentation/alctslita/*

13. Hopkins, Judith. "USMARC as a Metadata Shell," *Journal of Internet Cataloging*, 1999, vol. 2, no. 1, pp. 55-68.

14. Gorman, Michael. "Metadata or Cataloguing? A False Choice" *Journal of Internet Cataloging*, 1999, vol. 2, no. 1, pp. 5-22.

15. Caplan, Priscilla, and Rebecca Guenther. "Metadata for Internet Resources: The Dublin Core Metadata Elements Set and Its Mapping to USMARC," *Cataloging & Classification Quarterly*, 1996, vol. 22, no 3/4, pp. 43-58.

16. In the context of standards directly relevant to the CORC System, OCLC has voting or other representation in organizations that develop/maintain/govern: HTML, XML, RDF, MARC 21, UNIMARC, Unicode, and the Dublin Core Metadata Element Set.

17. Dublin Core/MARC/GILS Crosswalk: *http://lcweb.loc.gov/marc/dccross.html*

18. Some differences will be encountered for some records–CORC will not impose WorldCat's record size limits for example, and some data available in the Dublin Core view will not be visible in the MARC view (or part of the WorldCat record), but most users using most records will not notice significant differences in the metadata visible in OCLC-MARC form in the respective databases.

19. A 16 Feb. 2000 thread on CORC-L, CORC's electronic discussion list, summarizes OCLC's plans and references an administrative core proposal made by staff members of the Distributed Systems and Technology Centre and the National Library of Australia. See: *http://orc.rsch.oclc.org:5103/corc-l/msg00901.html*

20. Unicode home page: *http://www.unicode.org/*

Cataloging in CORC:
A Work in Progress

Jeff Edmunds
Roger Brisson

SUMMARY. In following a practice for developing software now common in the computing industry, OCLC has been developing CORC 'live,' allowing its customers, primarily libraries, to act as beta testers. This has allowed testers to provide continuous feedback as they use and interact with system features as they are added. This has also given beta testers, who have been predominantly catalogers, the unique opportunity to experience the latest computing technologies in a cooperative cataloging environment. Two catalogers from a large ARL library give a 'hands-on' report from the field, and, in so doing, provide a glimpse of what it is like to catalog Internet resources in CORC. *[Article copies available for a fee from The Haworth Document Delivery Service: 1-800-342-9678. E-mail address: <getinfo@haworthpressinc.com> Website: <http://www.HaworthPress.com>]*

KEYWORDS. CORC (Cooperative Online Resource Catalog), Dublin Core, metadata, library catalogs and cataloging, organization and control of Internet resources

INTRODUCTION

In announcing the CORC Project in the fall of 1998 as a major new initiative to harness the resources of libraries in cataloging the Internet,

Jeff Edmunds is Monographs Cataloging Specialist at the Pennsylvania State University, Pattee Library, University Park, PA 16801 (e-mail: jhe@psulias.psu.edu).

Roger Brisson is Digital Access Librarian at the Pennsylvania State University, Pattee Library, University Park, PA 16801 (e-mail: rob@psulias.psu.edu).

[Haworth co-indexing entry note]: "Cataloging in CORC: A Work in Progress." Edmunds, Jeff, and Roger Brisson. Co-published simultaneously in *Journal of Internet Cataloging* (The Haworth Information Press, an imprint of The Haworth Press, Inc.) Vol. 4, No. 1/2, 2001, pp. 89-109; and: *CORC: New Tools and Possibilities for Cooperative Electronic Resource Description* (ed: Karen Calhoun, and John J. Riemer) The Haworth Information Press, an imprint of The Haworth Press, Inc., 2001, pp. 89-109. Single or multiple copies of this article are available for a fee from The Haworth Document Delivery Service [1-800-342-9678, 9:00 a.m. - 5:00 p.m. (EST). E-mail address: getinfo@haworthpressinc.com].

OCLC invited libraries around the world to act as beta sites and to actively use the system as it was being developed by the staff of OCLC's Office of Research. Following a pattern long employed in the computer software industry, OCLC has effectively developed CORC 'live,' with its primary customers–libraries–interacting and providing feedback as work on the system has progressed. At the same time, in acting as beta sites, libraries have had the opportunity not only to let OCLC staff know what they liked and didn't like as new features were added to the system, but also to gain experience using state-of-the-art cataloging software in a cooperative environment. From its inception, OCLC has considered the CORC Project a testbed for developing the latest ideas and technologies in cooperative online cataloging. For catalogers, it has thus been possible to experience directly these new technologies in an actual production environment. While many of the innovations employed in the CORC system are applicable to a general cooperative cataloging environment, the CORC Project itself focuses on the cataloging of Internet resources. As such, many of the architectural features of CORC have been devised and optimized for creating 'metadata' records of Web sites. CORC is thus of interest to catalogers both because of its use of innovative cataloging technologies in general, and also because of the way it has been developing an interactive environment for cataloging Internet resources. Because of this perceived interest, this article has been devised as a concise 'report from the field,' providing a pragmatic glimpse at the Internet cataloging functionality of CORC as it is being developed by OCLC staff. The report is based on the active use of the system by two catalogers at a large ARL university, and is intended to be evaluative as well as descriptive. The two catalogers are members of a five-person task force charged with actively using CORC's record creation capabilities, and, in so doing to, assess its potential in being used for managing Internet resources at Penn State. For the purposes of the task force's charge, Internet resources are being selected by the task force members themselves, both for record creation and to study the nature of selecting Internet resources in a large research library. After briefly characterizing the CORC Project and its development up to the end of 1999 as it relates to its cataloging functionality, this essay will proceed with a step-by-step walk-through of the cataloging process in CORC.[1]

CORC AS A TESTBED FOR INNOVATION

From the beginning, OCLC has regarded CORC as an opportunity to bring together the results of a number of promising research projects into a single initiative. The technology behind its legacy database, the Online Union Catalog (OLUC), and the PRISM/Passport cataloging interface, stretch back over 20 years, making it difficult to implement all but the most incremental changes to these systems. A live cataloging environment, with thousands of daily transactions occurring to a database of well over 40 million records, has made it very challenging for OCLC staff to integrate the latest developments in computing and library technology. Catalogers have been eager to reap the benefits of the revolution in client-server computing that was introduced at the beginning of the 90s, and, with the latest generation of integrated library systems, growing numbers of catalogers can now make use of these technologies at the local level. More than ever, computing has the potential to automate many of the tedious activities in creating database records, and in so doing, to significantly rationalize much of the process of cataloging. Aware of this, over the past several years, OCLC's Office of Research has been working on a number of new projects of relevance to the cooperative cataloging environment. With the commercial development of its SiteSearch software suite, OCLC has been able to create cataloging tools employing the latest in Web-based computing technologies and to make these available to its library customer base. The foundation of the CORC system is the latest version of SiteSearch and its suite of cataloging and database management utilities. From the beginning of the CORC Project, OCLC has made it clear that, in addition to regarding CORC as a state-of-the-art system for creating metadata records of Internet resources, it also views the project as a testbed for possible future enhancements to WorldCat.[2]

Since CORC represents an entirely new cooperative cataloging environment, it has been possible for OCLC to rethink, from the ground up, the use of the latest computing technology in creating a new cataloging architecture. Many ideas long advocated by cataloging theorists, such as providing a flexible means of importing records in a variety of ways or in offering a highly configurable cataloging interface, could be pursued by OCLC programmers in developing CORC. That the programmers can quickly add or change features as beta testers suggest them is due to the fact that the interface has been developed using the Java programming language, which readily permits rapid development and changes to components of a program. The entire system is tightly integrated into the Web environment, as well as in making use of the latest features of a multitasking windowing operating system, thus allowing catalogers to make full use of the functionality of their desktop computers while creating records in CORC. Unfettered by legacy database technology, CORC programmers can use Java to provide catalogers with an extensive suite of enhancements to the basic record input and creation interface.

As one can surmise, configuring a cataloging environment optimized for the creation of metadata records for Internet resources leads to a noticeably different architecture and feature set than if devised for printed and other materials. In 'cataloging' Internet resources, it is not only possible, but necessary, to take advantage of the hyperlinking capability of the Web to include a direct hotlink to the cataloged resource. Maintaining the validity of this link (i.e., URL checking) becomes one of the important elements for resource control in the digital environment, and, as such, it poses significant technological challenges in developing the CORC system. In addition, since all Web pages possess header information in the page source code,[3] it is possible to automatically copy or "harvest" this information and use it as the basis for a cataloging record. If this source code is structured data found in identifiable fields, then much of the initial work of the cataloger could be automated. The potential of using structured data in this way is the driving force behind the creation of the Internet-specific descriptive data format known as Dublin Core. Most of the differences between print-based and Internet-based cataloging relate to the fact that, unlike online catalogs of printed material, there is an implied direct, integral relationship between the cataloging record and the actual item being cataloged in the realm of the Internet. If a database of cataloging records could be designed to reside 'natively' on the Internet, it would be possible to create a high degree of integration between such a catalog and the resources being described.

As a system that supports both MARC and Dublin Core and allows on-the-fly mapping of one standard to the other, CORC is an excellent tool for evaluating the two standards side by side. The relative merits of MARC and DC for describing online resources is a topic of lively discussion, but falls largely outside the scope of this article. In our section below on the practical aspects of cataloging in CORC, we will raise some of the issues and decisions the cataloger encounters as a result of the availability of the two standards and their co-existence in the same database. At Penn State, we have adopted Dublin Core as our tentative standard, based on what we see as its greater applicability to Internet resources and its relative ease of use.[4]

In creating CORC, OCLC is well aware that there would be a melding of two 'cultures' as the CORC cataloging community develops. On the one side, with a strong interest in providing an effective means of controlling Internet resources for users, OCLC's primary customer base of academic, public, special, and government libraries would bring a long tradition of cataloging experience and practices to the CORC Project. On the other side, computing and Internet specialists would be approaching the issues of Internet resource control from a strongly biased technological perspective. They would be more inclined to use evolving technologies to innovatively address the problems of resource control. Both 'cultures' are aware that the current generation of commercial search services, relying on a fully automated life cycle in metadata management, is insufficient in providing an effective means for users to find needed information. This latter approach relies heavily on the data harvesters to collect textual information from homepages (for gathering source data from the page headers), as well as in using sophisticated indexing software in developing large databases. CORC makes use of these and other cutting edge computing technologies, but its purpose is also to investigate and make optimal use of human intervention in adding structural and content-based value to cataloging records. It is hoped that the combination of the library cataloging tradition and innovative computing technologies will produce a system that is noticeably better than the existing search services.

This leads to an additional realm that represents a noteworthy difference between CORC and OCLC's traditional cooperative cataloging approach as represented in WorldCat. In order to insure a high degree of reliability and data integrity, a formal body of international policy and cataloging procedure has been developed around record creation in WorldCat. Complex descriptive cataloging rules, as represented in AACR2, as well as in following a consistent method in providing subject access to materials, as embodied in the Library of Congress subject cataloging manuals, have evolved to guarantee a high degree of consistency in the database. The complexity of these rules and procedures has played a dominant role in the development of workflows and the staffing or personnel structure necessary for record creation. Those involved in the development of CORC have proposed a relaxing of the rules and procedures that have been deemed necessary for printed and other materials, arguing that this degree of integrity and consistency will not be necessary for controlling Internet resources. Most would agree that this appears to be the case; the question, however, is how to determine how much control through rules and procedures will be necessary in the evolving CORC framework.

As of the fall of 1999, the CORC database included well over 200,000 records. This may seem a lot for some 100 libraries to have created in just a few months of beta testing, and, indeed, most of the records have come from earlier OCLC Internet cataloging projects, the most prominent being the InterCat Project and the NetFirst initiative.[5] The existing records represent a hodgepodge of data, varying widely in quality and completeness. Since the records are static and do not possess a dynamic relationship to the original resource, it can also be assumed that a large percentage of records are out-of-date and no longer include valid URLs. For this reason, relatively few CORC records have been created 'live' by CORC catalogers. Though OCLC has stressed that a strength of the CORC database is the relative quality of the resources represented because of their being deliberately 'selected' by librarians (as opposed to being automatically generated by a Web harvester), it is clear that the database includes a significant number of records relating to popular interests or trivial Websites, such as one would find in Yahoo! or the other commercial search services. While for certain types of searches CORC demonstrates precisely this principle of intelligent selection by providing results with a high degree of precision, because the database has yet to reach a critical mass of data (with records reaching into the millions, rather than in the hundreds of thousands), successful searching can still be inconsistent and spotty.

THE CORC CATALOGING ENVIRONMENT

The CORC environment will be familiar to catalogers accustomed to working in Windows and using a Web browser (see Figure 1). Cataloging in CORC occurs live on the Internet entirely within a browser interface (either Netscape 4.0 + or Internet Explorer 4.0 +). It is largely interactive and depends heavily on Java to achieve this level of dynamic interaction and responsiveness. The result is a readily configurable tool with a large complement of cataloging utilities, but one also subject to certain limitations imposed by the still novel character of the technology employed.[6]

The text of the records is entered directly into boxes within HTML forms, and drop-down menus allow the cataloger to add, remove, and edit fields, as well as verify headings, and finally to reformat, verify, and submit records.

FIGURE 1. The CORC cataloging entry screen.

Each such action necessitates a Java event and a reload of the screen from the CORC server. If Net traffic is high, this process can be tediously slow. Although some testers have reported unacceptably slow response times, in our testing here at Penn State, we have found that responsiveness is seldom slow enough to significantly impair productivity, though the constant refreshing of the Web display does require some patience on the part of the cataloger. Penn State, an Internet 2 institution, generally has access to wide bandwidth connections. To address the problems arising from Internet traffic for libraries with slow connections or for international cataloging agencies, OCLC has created a full-text data entry form which allows the cataloger to essentially enter all the data necessary to complete a record before entering it into the CORC system for reformatting and record validation. While not a permanent solution, it at least allows a wider spectrum of library types to participate in the CORC Project and makes for less frustration when the Net is particularly slow.

It should be repeated here that the CORC environment is in a state of continuous and considerable flux. As noted earlier, this is a first for OCLC–the "live" development of a project of this scope, with the testers directly involved in the evolution of the system. A significant advantage of the testers interacting with a system that relies on Java programming is that for many of its features changes and improvements can be made almost immediately. It has not been unusual during the course of the past year for improvements, based on suggestions posted to the CORC-L discussion list, to have been made to the system within hours. Details supplied here are based on the authors' own experience with the CORC database and interface as they existed from late summer to early winter, 1999.

CATALOGING IN CORC: A WALK-THROUGH

Record Creation

'Logging' into CORC is accomplished in the same way that one enters any password-protected Web site: the URL address to enter the CORC production system (*http://corc.oclc.org*) begins with a login id and password form. Once logged in, the cataloger is presented with four menus titled Search, Create, Show, and General. "Search" includes links to allow the cataloger to search both the CORC database (for records or for pathfinders), as well as the Library of Congress authorities indexes and Dewey indexes. "Create" links to pages for both record and pathfinder creation. "Show" allows the cataloger to view records organized by status, records previously 'tagged' by the cataloger for future reference, or usage statistics for the CORC system.

"General" includes items such as "Overview," "Administration," "Documentation," and "Display Options" (see Figure 1). Thus, in addition to providing access to the cataloging system itself, the CORC system, like the Library of Congress's *Cataloger's Desktop* CD-ROM, allows ready access to a suite of useful cataloging reference tools, such as the CORC documentation and user guides, and context-sensitive help system, and the LC authority files.

The cataloger generally begins by searching the database for records describing the resource he or she intends to catalog. Although a search function is invoked as part of the automated generation of records, the automated search has been found to be unreliable, frequently missing records already included in the database. If this manual search brings up no matches, indicating that the resource has not yet been cataloged, the cataloger may, as a preliminary step, have the system automatically generate a record based on the metadata contained in the resource's HTML header information and on the text of the resource itself. This is accomplished by entering the URL of the resource to be cataloged. At this stage, the cataloger also has the option of instructing the system to generate Dewey call numbers, possible subject keywords, and constant data as part of the automatically generated record (see Figure 2).

When this Web-based form is submitted, CORC searches the database for the URL string and returns a screen that lists the search results. If no records containing the URL have been found during this automated search, CORC returns a machine-generated preliminary record for the site and simultaneously loads the site into a new frame below the record at the bottom of the active window or, if the cataloger so chooses, into a new browser window. With both the resource and the record visible, the cataloger is then free to complete the record by modifying or deleting fields and by adding any fields lacking in the automatically generated record. MARC field numbers and indicators, or Dublin Core Element labels and qualifiers, as well as the contents of the fields themselves, are simply typed into boxes, as one would fill out any HTML form on the Web, and drop-down menus allow actions such as the insertion, deletion, or authority control of a given field. Generally, either ISBD punctuation or subfield delimiters can be entered as regular text within fields. In a procedure that will be familiar to users of WorldCat, records can be reformatted and automatically validated (checked for completion and correctness of syntax, constant data, etc.) before submission. At this point in the development of a CORC cataloging 'culture,' with no minimal standards in place for record completeness or accuracy in CORC, there is much greater freedom for the cataloger inputting records. Though formal discussion leading to implementation has yet to begin, CORC catalogers are aware that the establishment of minimal standards will be necessary to insure greater con-

FIGURE 2. The URL submission screen in CORC.

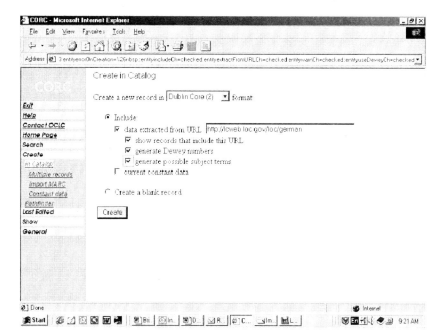

sistency of data. One downside of the Dublin Core standard is that, unlike MARC and AACR2, with their long history of development and exegetical addenda (LCRIs, etc.), DC is a young and still rapidly evolving approach to metadata that is not, properly speaking, yet a "standard." Throughout the beta development phase of CORC in 1999, a more syntactically complex form of Dublin Core, known as 'DC-Qualified' as opposed to the original simple or unqualified Dublin Core, was undergoing significant development. OCLC staff added the latest changes and revisions to the CORC cataloging interface as DC-Qualified progressed in its development, and, as this occurred, the mapping between MARC and DC-Qualified became noticeably more consistent and approaching a one-to-one correspondence with many of the MARC fields. It can be expected that this tendency will continue until DC-Qualified reaches the closing date before its first official release in the spring of 2000.

An additional feature of CORC that greatly simplifies multiple record creation in some cases is the 'Create multiple records' utility accessible through the initial record creation screen. If one wishes to catalog several resources available via the links on a single page (which is often the case when one has created a pathfinder), by giving the URL to this pathfinder or

Web page, this utility will go to the page, 'harvest' all of the active links on the page, and create initial CORC records of all the resources accessible through this page. While limited only to cases where a number of uncataloged resources are found as links on a Web page, this feature can save the cataloger a good deal of time in creating initial records of the resources made available by a pathfinder.

One frustrating aspect to using CORC is the lack of support for languages other than English. Though a Unicode-based upgrade to CORC was promised for last summer by the CORC staff, apparent problems in its implementation have delayed its appearance, and, as of January 2000, there is still no word from OCLC when the conversion to Unicode will take place. This makes the input of diacritics very cumbersome, and the antiquated method of using 'pipe' characters to designate a diacritic is still necessary in CORC. This also means that the diacritics must be manually, and tediously, converted to the corresponding non-diacritic characters for the automatically harvested data brought over from a Website when creating a new record.[7] The lack of diacritic support has been an embarrassment for OCLC, since, in recognizing the inherent global nature of the Internet, OCLC has, from the start, positioned CORC as an international project, inviting libraries from around the world to participate. Needless to say, in countries where English is not the primary language, CORC can only be used in a very limited way under these circumstances.

When the cataloger has completed, reformatted, and validated the record, it may be submitted to the stable database with one of several "status" values assigned to it: New, In-process, In-review, Private, and Complete. In a marked departure from the "master record" concept of OCLC's WorldCat, multiple records for the same resource may co-exist in CORC, and multiple versions of the *same* record can co-exist in different areas of the database, the Current and Archive subsystems.[8] However, in following a basic tenet for database architecture, like WorldCat, a one-to-one relationship between a record and its described resource should exist in the CORC *active*, or Current, database: principally, a particular resource should possess only a single record in the active database. Because data from a variety of sources make up the CORC database, multiple records are indeed present in significant numbers for a single resource, but, as in WorldCat, this should be considered undesirable and viewed in terms of a 'dirty' database. Because Internet resources represent the predominant type of material being described in CORC, the concept of granularity also plays an important role in the structure and nature of the database. This relates to the fact that in cataloging a Website the cataloger has the option of creating distinct records for multiple facets of a Website, depending on what the cataloger wishes to describe as a resource. This essentially represents the body of theory relating to analysis in bibliographic description, and it is noteworthy that, while it takes up only a few cursory pages in AACR2 (chapter 12), analysis becomes a central organizing principle when describing Internet resources. In CORC, a single 'Website' may then possess multiple records describing various resources found at the site, but this should not be regarded in terms of 'duplicate' records or faulty cataloging.[9]

An additional significant change from the master record concept is that a cataloger with authorized access to the database can edit any record, regardless of whether it was originally created at his or her institution. For example, if a record originally created by Cataloger A at Institution A is subsequently modified by Cataloger B at Institution B, the version of the record as modified by B will replace A's version in the current database, but A's version of the record is automatically archived and can be viewed by anyone who explicitly searches the Archive. The Archive thus contains a distinct record for each successive edited and submitted version of a given entity in the catalog. The database is searchable by status, as well as by institution, so a cataloger can easily generate a listing of all his or her institution's In-process or Complete records.

The fact that multiple records can co-exist in CORC raises the question of what 'holdings' mean in this online context, or of how institutions can place their imprimatur on cataloged resources so that users have some idea of whether a given institution has reviewed a resource and deemed it worthy of inclusion in their virtual collection. A holdings feature has been promised as an addition to the system in the near future. As of this writing, there is ongoing discussion about how such a feature should be implemented, since, in the online environment, holdings must be regarded in a 'virtual' sense and not as a resource that a library necessarily owns.

Automatically Generated Metadata

One of CORC's most powerful features is its ability to automatically generate a preliminary catalog record, which it accomplishes both by harvesting metadata imbedded in the <META> tag of the resource itself and by employing artificial intelligence techniques for analyzing the text of the resource and generating a series of possible keywords and/or Dewey call numbers based upon this analysis.

What becomes quickly apparent to anyone using this feature is that the quality of the record generated is directly proportional to the quality and extent of the metadata imbedded in the record and the clarity and concision of the text of the resource. Automatically generated Dewey call numbers are, as often as not, wildly inaccurate. WSKeywords, that is keywords generated by CORC based on an analysis of the text of the resource (rather than simply harvested from the any Subject.Keyword fields in the metadata included in the resource's <META> tags), tend to be too broad or too vague to be useful.[10] As of this writing, only a small minority of on-line resource creators routinely imbed metadata in their HTML files. It is to be anticipated, as authoring tools such as FrontPage, which includes a feature for easily imbedding metadata in documents, become more widely used, that metadata will become as common on the Internet as CIP in printed books. One also hopes that creators of on-line resources will become increasingly aware of the search and retrievability advantages of imbedding metadata in their documents.

One potential stumbling block for catalogers accustomed only to MARC is that, as of this writing, metadata tends to created with Dublin Core, rather than MARC, in mind. As mentioned above, CORC allows the cataloger to view any record in either MARC or DC format. Nearly every aspect of cataloging will be informed in some way by the MARC vs. DC question, and in many instances, at least at the present time, Dublin Core provides a more effective means for describing Internet resources whose very nature is fluid and sometimes ephemeral.

Although the mapping of DC-Qualified Elements to MARC fields is technologically a fairly straightforward process and one completed quickly and seamlessly by CORC, the conceptual differences between the two standards may create some confusion when, for example, the DC Element "Creator" in a resource's <META> tag is mapped to a MARC 100, field and this personal name does not seem to correspond to the usual AACR2 notion of a main entry, or when DC Element "Contributor.Corporate" is mapped to a 710 field, even though the corporate name in question may not be accounted for elsewhere in the descriptive fields of the record, as is current practice in MARC records conforming to AACR2 standards. Most creators of Web resources, if they include metadata at all in their documents, use DC as their standard and seldom have any familiarity with MARC or AACR2. Since DC is being specifically developed for describing Internet resources, and, conversely, since the first edition of AACR was originally created with printed book material as its primary object for description, and the second edition still betrays a strong 'bibliocentric' orientation, it stands to reason that using DC for describing Internet resources possesses numerous advantages. Overall, the authors found, in testing CORC and in developing a set of preliminary guidelines for the creation of records in the database, that Dublin Core is the preferable standard, both in terms of its applicability and its ease of use, partially because of DC's greater acceptance among non-catalogers and non-librarians in the Internet realm.[11]

Potential minor conceptual difficulties aside, the ability of CORC to automatically harvest metadata imbedded in documents is an extremely useful feature and promises to become even more useful as the interrelationship of

MARC and Dublin Core evolves and as more catalogers become familiar with, and potentially adopt, DC as a cataloging standard for Internet resources. The automatic generation of Dewey call numbers and possible subject keywords based on a textual analysis of the site can be a useful feature, but, as currently implemented, tends to generate more noise than useful information. Perhaps as AI techniques improve, so, too, will the usefulness of this feature. More information on subjects and call numbers is included later in this article. Something made possible by CORC's automatic metadata generation feature is that non-catalogers, such as selectors or bibliographers, can create minimal records in the database more easily than if strict MARC/AACR2 standards were not insisted upon.

Classification

As noted above, CORC allows the automatic generation of Dewey call numbers as part of the record creation process. Before even considering the use of Dewey, the cataloger is thus faced with a fundamental question in terms of the online environment: to classify or not to classify. Catalogers using MARC, and who are accustomed to cataloging electronic resources for their own institutional OPACs or in WorldCat, may adopt one of several methods for dealing with the question of classification. Some choose to assign classification as they would for any other print-based resources, using traditional LC or Dewey call numbers; some use free-form call numbers (e.g., "Electronic Resource") that serve as rudimentary collators of materials by type rather than subject. The question then becomes: Is classification useful, and worth the time, in an Internet environment?

It should be noted here, for those unfamiliar with Dublin Core, that there is no DC-Qualified element that deals specifically with classification. Dewey call numbers that appear in a Dublin Core record show up in *subject* fields–either Subject.DDC Local or Subject.DDC-Scorpion. Mapped to MARC, these two fields show up as 092 (Local Dewey call number) or 699 (Local subject heading), respectively. In a similar manner, the 050 maps to DC-Qualified as Subject.LCC, and the 090 maps as Subject.LCC Local. Thus, the use of Dewey or LC call numbers allows only for a "shelflist"-type collocation. In effect, the use of class numbers in the online environment becomes an additional, albeit alphanumeric, means of providing subject access for Internet resources. This function is clearly indicated in the automatic generation of multiple Dewey numbers for each resource, allowing the cataloger to use the numbers to provide access to particular facets or subject areas of the item being cataloged. Again, this deviates notably from the shelflist concept embodied in call numbers, emphasizing the subject-access nature of class numbers. Since classification schema like LCC construe the universe of knowledge based on a logical and hierarchical organization (typically deriving from academic disciplines), the relationships expressed are different than in the-saural schema such as LCSH. Providing access to relationships by this means can certainly be useful for searchers, the question the CORC community must address is whether the added effort in classifying Internet resources will lead to actual added value in searchers learning and making use of more complex schema like LCC. There is currently no automated support for LC call numbers within CORC (that is, catalogers can insert LC call numbers in records, which like Dewey numbers map to *subject* fields in Dublin Core, but LC numbers cannot be automatically generated, nor are the LC schedules consultable from within CORC the way the Dewey scheme is). Developers apparently found that, as a system of classification, Dewey was more complete, more concise, and clearer in its hierarchical structure than LC, making it better suited for implementation as part of an on-line catalog such as CORC.[12]

Penn State has provisionally adopted the practice of assigning the free-format call number "Electronic resource" or "Electronic journal" to on-line resources cataloged in its bibliographic database. This decision was made to provide a rudimentary collocation of all on-line resources held, or selected, by the Libraries. For records entered to the CORC database, given the unreliability of the automatically generated Dewey call numbers, the authors' own unfamiliarity with the Dewey scheme, and the questionable usefulness of traditional classification in an on-line catalog, we have chosen not to routinely classify resources.

Subject Terms

Subject terms can be added to a record in the usual manner and, if LCSH is the thesaurus being used, authority-checked from within CORC (more on this below).

The main conceptual difference between MARC and DC, with regard to subject terms, is that DC, unlike MARC, is more hospitable for uncontrolled subject keyword access in the form of a Subject.Keyword field (corresponding to MARC field 653, Index term, Uncontrolled, or 690, Local subject term). Although MARC has long had a 653 field available for uncontrolled subject terms, catalogers have come to heavily favor controlled access, whereas users of DC seem to be more amenable to using uncontrolled keywords. It should be noted, too, that if resource creators will some day be expected to routinely include metadata in the documents they create, the vast majority will adopt the practice of simply adding subject keywords rather than learning and consistently applying terms from a controlled (and constantly changing) thesaurus such as LCSH. As mentioned above, the CORC system can be instructed to generate possible subject terms as part of an automatically created preliminary record. If the resource's creator has included keywords in one or more <META> fields, these will be 'harvested' to a subject field in Dublin Core or to a 690 field if the cataloger is using the MARC standard. If no metadata subject terms have been included in the resource's header, CORC will generate one or (often) several keywords based on an analysis of the text of the resource itself, using rudimentary AI techniques. These are, more often than not, less than useful as subject terms. As an example, when CORC is instructed to generate subject terms for a website devoted to the California Guitar Trio, an acoustic music group, the terms it supplies are: "value," "informative articles," "message," "flag," and "control," hardly useful for retrieval. These terms, it turns out, were harvested from a JavaScript scrolling message that appears in the HTML source code for the web page. While there appears to be great potential in this realm of subject analysis and control, in its current iteration in CORC, it tends to create more work for the cataloger than if not used at all.

Because the commercial search engines most familiar to library users rely heavily on keyword searches for retrieval, because most metadata subject terms are simply keywords added by the resource's creator, and because current AI techniques are not equipped to generate controlled headings, the concept of subject access through uncontrolled terms is more prevalent on the Internet than in most library catalogs, where levels of heading control, even in the absence of formal authority control modules, has traditionally been relatively high. Given that assigning controlled headings is more time-consuming than supplying keywords and that nearly all online search engines rely heavily on keyword searches, catalogers of Internet resources may wish to consider whether, for some kinds of on-line materials, keyword access is preferable to traditional controlled heading analysis using LCSH (or another thesaurus), or whether keywords can be said to reasonably augment retrievability in certain cases. In other respects, assigning subjects in CORC is conceptually akin to doing so for traditional print materials.

Authority Control

Related to the issue of subject access is, of course, authority control. Another of CORC's powerful features is its ability to allow authority checking from within the record itself. The cataloger selects "Control" from a drop-down menu adjacent to the field being checked in the MARC view (name, title, or subject), and the LC authority file is automatically searched, with matches and near matches returned in a separate frame at the bottom of the browser window. Verified headings can be automatically inserted into the record by clicking a button. The valid form of the heading appears in the record as a hyperlink back to the authority record, and the drop-down menu beside the heading, as inserted into the bibliographic record, disappears as a reminder to the cataloger that this heading has been checked, is valid, and requires no further action. The heading can be edited, however, if, for example, the cataloger determines that the heading is valid but does not correspond to the person of the same name associated with the resource being cataloged.

The automatic authority checking feature is less useful in cases where no exact matches are found, and, as one could expect, this is a common occurrence for Internet resources. In similar manner, as of this writing there are too few records in the CORC database to do the same kind of bibliographic record checking one would do in WorldCat or RLIN in establishing the form(s) of name most commonly used by a given person or corporate entity, in keeping with NACO standards. In late 1999, OCLC added a browsing feature for the authority file which significantly enhanced the advantages of having an authority system closely integrated into the cataloging module.

As yet there is no authority control feature (i.e., cross-references) as part of the search feature of CORC. This would be of little use, of course, in a database that supports not only multiple thesauri but also uncontrolled keyword subject terms. It remains to be seen what kind of authority control features develop in light of the more flexible approach to cataloging occurring in the realm of Internet resources. As with automatically generated metadata, automated authority control is another area in which technological advances may permit the creation of robust systems capable of providing useful levels of consistency at a minimum investment of human intervention and system resources. For the moment, however, keyword searching and rudimentary AI techniques have the upper hand in the Internet environment.

COMPLETING THE RECORD

Once it has been completed to a cataloger's satisfaction, a record can be reformatted (removing unused fields and the like) and validated much as in WorldCat. With a scroll-menu, the cataloger can then submit the record to the database, but, before being added, it appears once again as a Web-formatted record (see Figure 3). With this screen, the cataloger has the option of sending the record with *complete* status to the stable, or active, database, or, alternatively, to mark and submit the record with a *Private, New, In-Process,* or *In-Review* status. These additional status designations permit a cataloger (or a cataloging institution) to effectively set up distinctive workflows when using the CORC system. Non-professional catalogers, for example, could create initial records in CORC and save them to the In-Process queue, where trained staff or catalogers could later bring up the records for more comprehensive cataloging. CORC allows an institution to call up all the records in each of these status queues, thus making it possible to efficiently manage the creation of metadata for CORC. One can expect that OCLC will further develop this concept, along with continuing to refine the status designations

FIGURE 3. Completing the CORC Record.

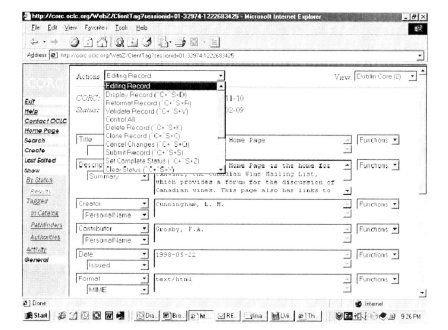

for records input, before CORC is officially 'released' as a service some time in 2000.

PROBLEMS AND OTHER ISSUES STILL TO BE ADDRESSED IN CORC

Anyone using the system will notice relatively quickly the two most obvious shortcomings when considering its use in a full production-level environment: the sometimes slow response time due to Internet traffic and the intermittent bugginess of browser/server interaction. While neither shortcoming should be lightly dismissed, each has the potential for being greatly mitigated in the foreseeable future, and, in fact, a number of incremental improvements relating to these issues have been made in the past six months. During our interaction with the system, the authors found slowness an infrequent problem; browser bugginess, too, was infrequent, but when it did occur, it could be so serious as to prevent cataloging (for example, when screen reloads failed to supply the correct text boxes and/or pull-down menus). The Java environment, which carries out much of the interactive computing on the user's client PC, makes it very challenging for the OCLC programmers working on CORC to isolate and debug program glitches, since it is possible that problems occur when the CORC software interacts with software on the user's client PC (such as the particular version and configuration of the user's Web browser).

Less obvious, but still notable potential weaknesses, are the quantity and quality of records in the database. As of this writing, CORC includes approximately 216,000 records, many of which are legacy records from earlier OCLC Internet cataloging projects, such as the NetFirst initiative. The quality of the records, as well of the quality of the Internet resources they describe, vary widely, both because the earlier initiatives were often experimental in nature and lacked rigid selection and cataloging standards and because CORC itself, still in the development stage, has no such standards in place. Many of the legacy records are of dubious quality (minimal records with inaccurate information), describe resources of questionable value to libraries, and/or contain invalid URLs. Whether CORC will someday be seen by users as a superior alternative to more traditional commercial search engines such as Yahoo! or Google depends largely on the size and quality of the database. If the database is too small and too highly selective, CORC risks being too specialized to be useful for the average academic user. If the database is too large and too lax in its standards for selection and cataloging, it risks being indistinguishable from other search engines. An optimal balance must be found between size, quality, and comprehensiveness. Based on impressionistic feedback from CORC users, at the present time, it would appear that scientific and engineering fields are well represented in CORC and the humanities less so.

The size of the database is, of course, a function of the level of participation by libraries and other cataloging institutions. Until a significant number of institutions adopt CORC as their de facto Internet catalog and contribute significant numbers of records, CORC risks being seen as unnecessary duplication of local efforts to catalog Internet resources in institutional OPACs.[13] The quality of the database is a function of many things, including the existence of selection and cataloging standards. Also an issue is the co-existence in CORC of records created according to both Dublin Core and MARC cataloging standards. Though not necessarily true in all cases, Dublin Core records tend to be simpler and to conform to less rigid standards than MARC records, whose field designations stress a high degree of descriptive precision. In a database of Internet resources, issues of authority control and cataloging quality will almost certainly have to be seen in less stringent terms than many catalogers are accustomed to if CORC is to become an up-to-date and reasonably comprehensive resource for locating Internet resources.

From a cataloger's perspective, many of the most important improvements to the system yet to be implemented are those that were discussed at the CORC Participants' meeting in Dublin, Ohio in November, 1999. The question of documentation was addressed by OCLC shortly after the meeting, and now the CORC site includes extensive manuals in PDF format that are very helpful for the user new to the system.[14] Minimum standards of cataloging have yet to be developed, although individual institutions and working groups have been hard at work on crafting preliminary guidelines for cataloging in CORC. This, of course, is a task more for the cataloging community at large than for OCLC, which, during the development stage of CORC, has been allowing the testers to come to their own conclusions about what levels of standards and quality control are appropriate for a catalog of Internet resources.

On the system side, the most important enhancements that have yet to be implemented, and are of primary relevance to the cataloger, include consistent and reliable URL checking, Unicode support, integration and/or interface of the CORC database with WorldCat, and the implementation of a 'holdings' feature akin to the holdings symbol feature of WorldCat.

One of the most challenging aspects in creating a comprehensive and accurate catalog of Internet resources is that such resources are inherently more dynamic than print-based materials. For a catalog of this kind to be useful, its links to the resources it describes must be reliable. A rudimentary URL checking feature currently exists in CORC, whereby an institution can call up a list of all the resources it has cataloged for which the URL was found to be invalid. It is then up to the cataloger to investigate, determine whether the resource has vanished or simply moved, and to update the catalog record. As of this writing, the URL checker is not run regularly, so records that have had their URLs manually updated to be correct will still show up as having invalid URLs. CORC developers have stated that URL checking is still undergoing development and testing, and, eventually, the URL checker will be run more frequently, which will go a long way toward easing the concerns of catalogers.

One of the fundamental questions of interest to catalogers is the relationship of CORC with OCLC's WorldCat. As stated earlier, CORC can be seen as a testbed for many of the technological innovations that might someday be incorporated into WorldCat or its successor databases. Many wonder whether CORC records will be routinely loaded into WorldCat (or vice versa), or whether the CORC interface and cataloging system will, in some sense, replace WorldCat, thereby becoming a comprehensive database that includes records not only for traditional media but for Internet resources as well. A possible scenario, in terms of current technological development, is that the CORC cataloging system will become the primary record creation tool for all OCLC databases, and that records will be sent or tagged for specific format-related databases. OCLC has already announced that a relationship between WorldCat and CORC records is being established by providing each CORC record with a unique WorldCat record number, thus allowing the records to interact with one another.

An allied issue is the concept of holdings. The WorldCat master record concept allows individual institutions to attach holdings to a record to let the world know that it owns the item described. For Internet resources, which are not normally thought of as physically residing at a particular location, the holdings concept must be modified somewhat, but most institutions agree that being able to add their 'imprimatur' to a given CORC record (to signify that institution has reviewed the resource described and, in effect, formally 'selected' it for inclusion in its collection) must be a feature of CORC in order for the database to be seen as a useful collection development resource by bibliographers, selectors, and collection development managers. While appearing to be a simple concept to realize, a number of issues will need to be worked out, such as allowing multiple URLs to reside with the same record in cases where a particular product (or 'work' in the Internet sense) can be found at numerous locations. A common example of this is where more than one institution has purchased a digital resource and has mounted it locally on an in-house server.[15]

CONCLUSION

As an experimental project and a work in progress, CORC has immense potential for allowing libraries to cooperatively tackle one of the most daunting tasks of the new century: organizing and providing some measure of controlled access to the vast quantity of electronic resources now available via the Internet. OCLC is to be lauded for its success in coordinating so many individuals and institutions in this huge effort and for its willingness to develop a system "live," with the library world not only watching, but interacting with the system, spotting bugs, suggesting changes, and generally providing continuous (and no doubt sometimes tiring) feedback to the system's developers. If the system does realize its potential, it will be largely due to the hard work, creativity, and persistence of all the people involved, most notably OCLC's seemingly tireless programmers.

NOTES

1. Background information on the Penn State CORC Taskforce can be found at: http://www.personal.psu.edu/faculty/r/o/rob1/corc/

2. OCLC maintains an extensive Website for CORC. General background information on the CORC Project can be found at: http://www.oclc.org/oclc/corc/about/about.htm

3. Other than an automatically generated title (and perhaps the name of the page creator), very few Web pages currently possess useful descriptive metadata. The intent in making a standard like Dublin Core a simple one to learn is to foster the use of metadata by authors themselves in describing their Websites.

4. See the official Dublin Core Website for additional information on this evolving standard (*http://purl.org/dc/*).

5. The InterCat database contributed approximately 50,000 records to CORC, and NetFirst around 100,000 records. The latter service began in 1996 and is currently available in WorldCat as a database of Internet resources that presents to the user concise, index-like records.

6. An overview, along with functional requirements, of cataloging in CORC can be found at: *http://www.oclc.org/oclc/corc/ppt/199910/1099corccatattrain.ppt*

7. See the chapter "Insert Diacritics and Special Characters" in the Edit Records part of the CORC System User Guide for a full description of how to insert diacritics in CORC. As noted, diacritic insertion is similar to the older OCLC Prism system, where a character string with pipes represents the diacritic. For example, the German word *täglich* would be represented as 't|um|aglich' in CORC. As one could surmise, this has not endeared CORC to the many academic catalogers in North America or in those countries with languages possessing diacritics, who must manually convert all the diacritics taken from a Website to the piped character form necessary for the CORC database.

8. At meetings during the 2000 ALA Midwinter Meeting in San Antonio, OCLC announced it would be implementing some form of the Master Record concept in the production version of CORC, but it was unclear at this early stage exactly how this would be structured in CORC.

9. An interesting exposition of granularity can be found in Carl Lagoze's "From Static to Dynamic Surrogates," *D-Lib Magazine,* June 1997 (*http://www.dlib.org/dlib/june97/06lagoze.html*).

10. See *http://orc.rsch.oclc.org:5061/* for a general description of the OCLC WordSmith Project.

11. A list of general articles and other resources on Dublin Core can be found at Penn State's CORC Taskforce Website: *http://www.personal.psu.edu/faculty/r/o/rob1/corc/dublin_core_resources.htm*

12. See current OCLC research using DDC for classifying Web resources at its Knowledge Organization Research Website: *http://www.oclc.org:5047/~vizine/kor/index.htm*

13. As of the fall 1999 CORC meeting, there were well over 100 institutional participants from around the world, and the number was growing rapidly. Most of the participants were academic libraries, with a significant number of government libraries also involved.

14. See the CORC Documentation page at: *http://www.oclc.org/oclc/corc/documentation/index.htm*

15. A brief summary of the important issues discussed at the fall 1999 CORC meeting, composed by one of the authors of the present article, can be found at: *http://www.personal.psu.edu/faculty/r/o/rob1/corc/fall1999meeting.htm*

Utilizing CORC to Develop
and Maintain Access
to Biomedical Web Sites

Norm Medeiros
Robert F. McDonald
Paul Wrynn

SUMMARY. The need for robust access to scholarly Internet-based information is great. Existing search engines cannot filter the gems from the sand, nor do their algorithms provide adequate precision for retrieval.[1] OCLC's Cooperative Online Resource Catalog (CORC) attempts to bring an OPAC-like standardization to the non-standard world that is

Norm Medeiros is Technical Services Librarian at New York University School of Medicine, and authors "On the Dublin Core Front," a column appearing quarterly in *OCLC Systems & Services*. He will be a presenter at the 2000 ALA preconference, "Metadata: Libraries and the Web–Retooling AACR and MARC21 for Cataloging in the Twenty-First Century" (e-mail: medeiros@library.med.nyu.edu).

Robert F. McDonald is Associate Director of Collection Services at the Ehrman Medical Library at the New York University. This division is responsible for the selection, acquisition, and bibliographic control of all resources, regardless of format, provided by the library (e-mail: mcdonald@library.med.nyu.edu).

Paul Wrynn is Collection Development Librarian at New York University School of Medicine, has published in the *Bulletin of the Medical Library Association,* and frequently delivers presentations. His newest presentation, "Are Dragons Really Free? A Comparative Study of the Costs of Online Journal Access," will be delivered at the Annual Meeting of the Medical Library Association in May 2000 (e-mail: wrynn@library.med.nyu.edu).

The authors wish to thank John Riemer for his thoughtful editorial suggestions.

[Haworth co-indexing entry note]: "Utilizing CORC to Develop and Maintain Access to Biomedical Web Sites." Medeiros, Norm, Robert F. McDonald, and Paul Wrynn. Co-published simultaneously in *Journal of Internet Cataloging* (The Haworth Information Press, an imprint of The Haworth Press, Inc.) Vol. 4, No. 1/2, 2001, pp. 111-121; and: *CORC: New Tools and Possibilities for Cooperative Electronic Resource Description* (ed: Karen Calhoun, and John J. Riemer) The Haworth Information Press, an imprint of The Haworth Press, Inc., 2001, pp. 111-121. Single or multiple copies of this article are available for a fee from The Haworth Document Delivery Service [1-800-342-9678, 9:00 a.m. - 5:00 p.m. (EST). E-mail address: getinfo@haworthpressinc.com].

the Internet. Since the beginning of the CORC research project in January 1999, emphasis has necessarily been placed on technical development, such as the mapping between MARC and Dublin Core, the export function, and the META tag builder. However, the appeal and value for CORC participation among libraries lies ultimately with what it can mean for library users. The library can use CORC to select sites that offer quality content. The library patron is served by being able to go effortlessly to the exact resource needed and can avoid sifting through search engine results that often consist of pages of irrelevant links. Standard CORC features, such as authority control for name access, assist with resource location. Features on the horizon include URL maintenance for greater accuracy of records and enhanced design options to assist with aesthetically pleasing displays of search results. CORC records can be utilized in many ways to assist library patrons' resource discoveries. Possibilities include MARC record exporting from CORC to a library's OPAC, creating pathfinders that can be downloaded to a library's Web site or held remotely on the CORC server, and the ability to use CORC as a publicly accessible database. The Ehrman Medical Library, New York University School of Medicine, has developed its vision for best utilizing CORC in terms of patron needs, staff involvement, and emerging trends in Web development. *[Article copies available for a fee from The Haworth Document Delivery Service: 1-800-342-9678. E-mail address: <getinfo@haworthpressinc.com> Website: <http://www.HaworthPress.com>]*

KEYWORDS. CORC, metadata, Dublin Core, Web development

INTRODUCTION

Hundreds of millions of pages exist on the World Wide Web. Until recently, in order to provide access to quality Web content, libraries needed to create and maintain lists mounted locally. Link checking, if done at all, was time-consuming and reactive by nature. The larger task of locating scholarly information on the Internet was equally imposing. To assist with resource selection, the CORC database offers a level of quality and supports cooperative efforts that help streamline the resource discovery process.[2]

THE WAY WE WERE

Prior to joining the CORC research project in July 1999, the Ehrman Medical Library maintained subject-specific pages referred to as "Biomedical Sites by Subject." These pages were categorized according to the National Library of Medicine's Medical Subject Headings (MeSH) and listed freely-available Web sites selected for quality of content. A three-member Web team administered these 100+ pages, and, although link checking was performed on a bi-weekly basis, the content of these pages quickly grew stale. Simply put, the upkeep was impossible for three librarians to effectively maintain on a local level. Attention was, instead, directed toward databases and the journal literature, the cost-imperative being a dominating factor, as well as the heavy use of these standard tools in biomedical libraries. "Web sites," as separate from e-journal or database sites, were a new model, without precedent and in many cases without considerable content, guarantees, or even expectations. The growth of Web sites as mediums in themselves leads to the need to seek out those which actually do offer scholarly content.

STATISTICS DON'T LIE

Monthly log statistics indicated a very low level of use for the "Biomedical Sites by Subject" pages.[3] Although it cannot be determined that the relatively poor upkeep of these pages was the reason for their low usage, it was apparent that our patrons deserved a better product, especially considering the immensity of information available online.

A MODEST PROPOSAL

Motivation for the Ehrman Medical Library's decision to apply for inclusion in the CORC project was two-fold:

- To contribute metadata records to the database, and thus to our other CORC collaborators;
- To gain a level of quality in the creation and maintenance of "Biomedical Sites by Subject" pages.

In order to achieve this second goal, the authors believed a new procedure for administering the "Biomedical Sites by Subject" pages was required. Our proposal divides the 100+ biomedical subjects by the professional staff, thus making each librarian responsible for approximately seven to nine subject areas. Using CORC, the existing "Biomedical Sites by Subject" pages, and other means of review, each librarian identifies quality resources and checks to see if records for these are available in the CORC database. Resources not represented in CORC are described and documented within an in-house Web form, the results of which are sent to the CORC Cataloging Team (CCT).

FIGURE 1. Access page to subject-specific Web pages, categorized according to the National Library of Medicine's *List of Journals Indexed* subject headings.

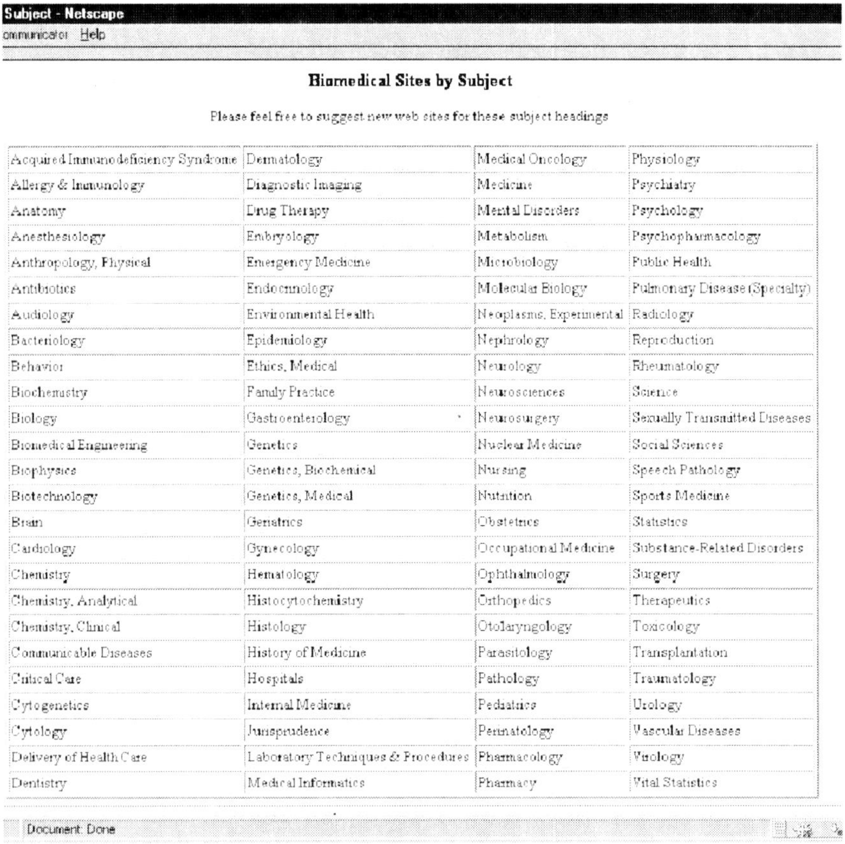

Biomedical Sites by Subject

Please feel free to suggest new web sites for these subject headings

Acquired Immunodeficiency Syndrome	Dermatology	Medical Oncology	Physiology
Allergy & Immunology	Diagnostic Imaging	Medicine	Psychiatry
Anatomy	Drug Therapy	Mental Disorders	Psychology
Anesthesiology	Embryology	Metabolism	Psychopharmacology
Anthropology, Physical	Emergency Medicine	Microbiology	Public Health
Antibiotics	Endocrinology	Molecular Biology	Pulmonary Disease (Specialty)
Audiology	Environmental Health	Neoplasms, Experimental	Radiology
Bacteriology	Epidemiology	Nephrology	Reproduction
Behavior	Ethics, Medical	Neurology	Rheumatology
Biochemistry	Family Practice	Neurosciences	Science
Biology	Gastroenterology	Neurosurgery	Sexually Transmitted Diseases
Biomedical Engineering	Genetics	Nuclear Medicine	Social Sciences
Biophysics	Genetics, Biochemical	Nursing	Speech Pathology
Biotechnology	Genetics, Medical	Nutrition	Sports Medicine
Brain	Geriatrics	Obstetrics	Statistics
Cardiology	Gynecology	Occupational Medicine	Substance-Related Disorders
Chemistry	Hematology	Ophthalmology	Surgery
Chemistry, Analytical	Histocytochemistry	Orthopedics	Therapeutics
Chemistry, Clinical	Histology	Otolaryngology	Toxicology
Communicable Diseases	History of Medicine	Parasitology	Transplantation
Critical Care	Hospitals	Pathology	Traumatology
Cytogenetics	Internal Medicine	Pediatrics	Urology
Cytology	Jurisprudence	Perinatology	Vascular Diseases
Delivery of Health Care	Laboratory Techniques & Procedures	Pharmacology	Virology
Dentistry	Medical Informatics	Pharmacy	Vital Statistics

The "Biomedical Web Site Form" provides boxes into which information can be typed or pasted. The 15 Dublin Core elements are represented, but only three fields are required for a complete record: URL, Description, and MeSH Heading.[4] The URL is the data against which CORC checks for matching records. Additionally, the URL is used by the CORC harvester when creating a new record. Description was deemed vital, since this field of information follows a hotlinked title in a CORC pathfinder. This information should give users a sound understanding of the Web site's scope. Finally, at least one Medical Subject Heading was mandated since CORC pathfinders

FIGURE 2. Form used by subject bibliographers. Data entered is sent to the CORC Cataloging Team (CCT).

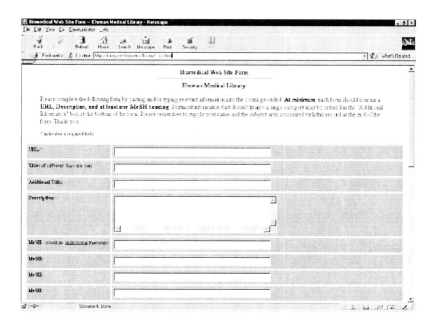

created by Ehrman librarians would be based on these particular subject areas.

Using a complete "Biomedical Web Site Form," the CCT, comprised of staff from the Bibliographic Control Department, enters a Dublin Core metadata record for the site into CORC, after which the librarian is notified that her resource is ready for tagging. The librarian returns to CORC, tags desired resources, creates the pathfinder, and e-mails the pathfinder's URL to the Web team. The Web team places the link to the CORC pathfinder on the "Biomedical Sites by Subject" page, in effect replacing access to the original subject page. It is expected that upkeep of the CORC pathfinder would be continual, though, at present, procedures for such maintenance have not been proposed.

WHAT TO SELECT

The Ehrman Medical Library's efforts to offer access to resources in electronic format are great. Access to over 800 electronic journals is available both from the Web site and the online catalog. Likewise, electronic texts, newer acquisitions for the library, also are represented on the Web site and within the OPAC. It is considered essential by the authors that CORC pathfinders supplement, not replicate, the efforts being performed in these areas. Users benefit by having the best Web sites available, without clutter from such duplication. Web site log statistics show that e-journals, especially, are sought after by patrons as a discrete category in the area of the biomedical sciences. Therefore, it is proposed that resources selected in CORC be limited to the following resource types:

- Homepages of professional societies
- Major sections from the Web site of a professional society that offer considerable content within a MeSH subject area
- Pages from professionals with established credentials in a given specialty or field
- Pages that offer cases, transcripts of cases, protocols, practice guidelines, and other resources in the field
- NYU Medical Center sites

In a similar fashion, certain resource types were eliminated from CORC contention:

- Sites that offer no content but merely take users to a list of links;
- Sites where the credentials of those responsible for the content cannot be established;
- Sites of local interest only (exceptions are made for NYU pages);
- Sites the library cannot access due to payment requirements;[5]
- E-Journals, since these are included on the library's Web site, and are accessible via crosswalks;
- E-Texts, since these are included on the library's Web site, and are accessible via crosswalks;
- Databases, since these are included on the library's Web site.

CORC 101: WHAT SELECTORS NEED TO KNOW

As noted earlier, a catalyst for the Ehrman Medical Library's decision to join CORC was the need to enhance its existing "Biomedical Sites by Subject" area, pages that list quality, freely available Web content. However, CORC houses much more than this subset of resources. Since CORC was initially seeded with records from NetFirst and InterCat, many records exist in the database for commercial resources, especially electronic journals, which do not fit our selection criteria for "Biomedical Sites by Subject."

FIGURE 3. A completed pathfinder, as it appears on the CORC server.

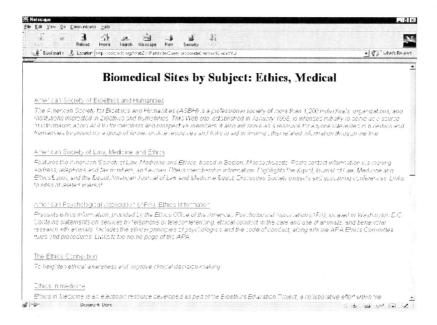

Another pitfall to selection includes record duplication. Because Web pages are malleable and not as clear-cut in their layout as materials in traditional formats, a degree of duplication exists within the CORC database. Contributors may differ in their opinion of a resource's title. For instance, should the title of a Web page be what displays at the top of the screen or what the author included within the opening and closing <TITLE> tags in the HTML source document? Such duplicates may not be immediately recognizable to a searcher. CORC's URL checker may catch some duplicates before harvesting metadata during the creation process, but it cannot, at present, detect the sameness that exists between mirrored sites. Selectors need to caution themselves against these scenarios or risk including duplicates in their pathfinders.

COMPETING VOCABULARIES

As of October 1999, there were over 150 institutions participating in CORC. However, only a handful of these have a medical affiliation. MeSH is the authority on which subject pathfinders are created at the Ehrman Medical Library. Since MeSH terms don't always have a one-to-one relationship with other predominant subject vocabularies, such as the Library of Congress, subject searches in CORC may not result in accurate retrieval. For example, a subject search in CORC on the MeSH heading *Substance-Related Disorders* results in 19 hits. A subject search on the LC heading *Substance Abuse* yields 177 hits. An additional search on the related LC heading *Drug Abuse* results in 244 records. Perhaps the biggest obstacle OCLC faces in regard to CORC's success is reconciling the conflicts between various subject vocabularies. In the future, authority control may provide some assistance to searchers, but even this may prove inadequate since some terms may not be cross-referenced. For now, Ehrman librarians will need to identify synonyms for their subject areas and search CORC against these terms in addition to their authorized MeSH subject headings. A level of subject expertise will be required in order to secure maximum retrieval in performing CORC searches.

A WEB TEAM'S VIEW OF CORC

As noted earlier, the Ehrman Medical Library Web team was solely responsible for creating and updating the "Biomedical Sites by Subject" pages. Construction of these pages was prompted by the creation of a subject-specific e-journal page. The immediate need to mount a "Biomedical Sites by Subject" page proved more challenging. Without the print equivalents and means of review found for e-journals and databases, the selection process for Web sites was comparatively rudderless. As the number of subject pages expanded, time was taken from the maintenance on existing pages. As a result of CORC, the Web team's burden has been greatly relieved. Maintenance of subject-specific pages is divided by the professional staff, and dynamic link-checking and correction are in the cards as future enhancements to CORC. Because of this latter feature, the decision to keep pathfinders on the CORC server was made, despite the loss of some design capabilities.

WHY DUBLIN CORE?

Library OPACs are no longer the single method of resource discovery available in academic libraries. They now compete with databases offering direct access to fulltext, such as MEDLINE and Web of Science, as well as with general search engines, such as Yahoo and AltaVista. Nowhere is this truer than in academic medical libraries, where the greatest numbers of catalog searches are performed simply to check journal holdings.[6]

CORC eliminates the need for adding MARC records to OPACs for online resources that are freely available. The result is a trend towards MARC bibliographic records for electronic resources to represent only those pur-

FIGURE 4. An expanded Dublin Core view of the CORC record for CARDIAX, a product of the University of Michigan Medical School.

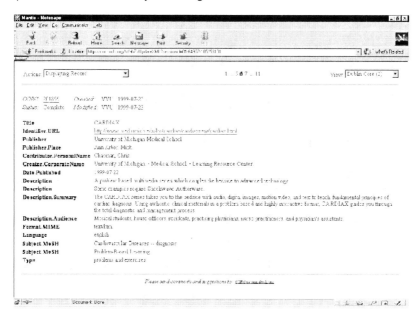

chased or those based on print models, such as journals, books, bibliographies and indexes. CORC records are created to describe these freely available Web-sites. The Dublin Core standard is used because it allows a broader group of staff to enter records into the CORC database, because it is more flexible, because it allows for faster input and because it is specifically designed for the description of electronic resources. Dublin Core, an international metadata standard comprised of 15 elements, offers adequate description capabilities without the strict indicator values, fixed fields, and punctuation mandated by the MARC format. Qualified Dublin Core metadata offers enhanced agents for a greater level of description, more than suitable for patron needs.

SUBJECT APPROACH TO WEB DEVELOPMENT

Discussion on the CORC listserv indicates that many libraries are entering records into CORC in the MARC format and exporting these to their OPACs. This process perpetuates the traditional access points provided by the online catalog. However, the role of the OPAC is diminishing as search engines gain favor with library users. Moreover, the proliferation of electronic versions of

FIGURE 5. Links to other subject-specific resources, as displayed at the bottom of a CORC pathfinder.

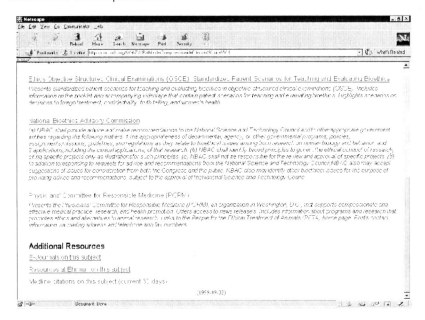

print materials is slowly creating the long-awaited "virtual library." The Ehrman Medical Library Web team believes organization of these resources is best achieved using a subject approach. The online catalog is not soon likely to become a repository of journal citations. Likewise, it cannot provide access to much of the best Web-based content, since cataloging is such a costly endeavor. Therefore, the Web team has experimented with subject-specific "crosswalks." In this approach, users select their subject interest, and have the option to view e-journals, e-texts (when available), Web sites, online catalog (MEDCat) resources, and recent Medline citations on that particular subject.

Administration of these crosswalks is practically maintenance-free since the individual resources are either dynamically updated or URLs unlikely to change. In this subject approach to resource discovery, the Web site becomes the most prominent research tool for library patrons.

PERSONAL CUSTOMIZATION: CORC A LA CARTE

Personal customization of Web sites is becoming a standard feature of many sites. Most search engines, including Yahoo and Excite, offer users the ability to add links to their homepage, resulting in a more useful and specific page. Along these lines, the Ehrman Medical Library is creating customization options using the MyLibrary software, available from North Carolina State University Libraries.[7] MyLibrary uses the MySQL database server to allow users the ability to move links of their choosing up to the homepage. During this preliminary phase, e-journals, e-texts, and Web sites are being moved into the structured query language (SQL) database so that users will have the ability to extract these for inclusion on their personal section of the Ehrman Medical Library homepage. At present, CORC pathfinders are being exported, brought into the SQL database, and singled out in order to be selected by users on an individual basis.

BENEFITS TO LIBRARY USERS

There is little question that the quality of pathfinders we propose is far greater than those currently maintained. The assignment of subject areas to librarians broadens the pool of qualified bibliographers and hastens the creation process. Library patrons at other participating CORC institutions will also benefit from the quality of these contributed records. Moreover, detailed links to better Web content adorn our CORC pathfinders. In time, dynamic URL and description maintenance between CORC records and pathfinders will make our efforts even more worthwhile.

REFERENCES

1. See Clifford Lynch's "Searching the Internet." *Scientific American*, v. 276, no. 3 (Mar. 1997).

2. See description of CORC's mission available on the Internet at *http://www.oclc.org/oclc/research/projects/corc/*

3. The average number of hits on a "Biomedical Sites by Subject" page, according to the October 1999 log, was 16. By comparison, the average number of hits on an "E-Journals by Subject" page for the same period was 20. The average number of hits on an "E-Journals by Title" page is 319.

4. The title is automatically harvested during the creation process.

5. Included are members-only areas of professional society sites or commercial sites to which the library has not purchased access.

6. Approximately one-third of all searches performed on the Ehrman Medical Library catalog are for journal title.

7. For more information, connect to the MyLibrary web site at *http://my.lib.ncsu.edu/*

Never the Twain Shall Meet?
Collaboration Between Catalogers
and Reference Librarians in the OCLC
CORC Project at Brown University

Ann Caldwell
Dominique Coulombe
Ronald Fark
Michael Jackson

SUMMARY. In the spring of 1999, the Brown University Library became a participant in the CORC project. The reference department had two goals that had been difficult to achieve due to time constraints and workloads. One was the creation of subject pathfinders by reference librarians; the other goal was developing a mechanism for alerting our end users to quality Web sites and print sources. In addition, the catalog department had the goal of exposing more staff, both professional and paraprofessional, to cataloging Internet resources. The ease of creating bibliographic records and the ability to develop pathfinders in the CORC Project has helped break down the reluctance of reference librarians to "catalog" records and has fostered collaboration between cataloging

Ann Caldwell is Bibliographic Control Coordinator and Principal Cataloger, Brown University Library.

Dominique Coulombe is Head of the Catalog Department, Brown University Library.

Ronald Fark is Head of the Reference Department, Brown University Library (e-mail: Ronald_Fark@brown.edu).

Michael Jackson is the Social Sciences Reference/Collection Development Librarian, Brown University Library.

[Haworth co-indexing entry note]: "Never the Twain Shall Meet? Collaboration Between Catalogers and Reference Librarians in the OCLC CORC Project at Brown University." Caldwell et al. Co-published simultaneously in *Journal of Internet Cataloging* (The Haworth Information Press, an imprint of The Haworth Press, Inc.) Vol. 4, No. 1/2, 2001, pp. 123-130; and: *CORC: New Tools and Possibilities for Cooperative Electronic Resource Description* (ed: Karen Calhoun, and John J. Riemer) The Haworth Information Press, an imprint of The Haworth Press, Inc., 2001, pp. 123-130. Single or multiple copies of this article are available for a fee from The Haworth Document Delivery Service [1-800-342-9678, 9:00 a.m. - 5:00 p.m. (EST). E-mail address: getinfo@haworthpressinc.com].

123

and reference staff. A plan of implementation and training was put into place. The plan involved the establishment of a small team of volunteers from cataloging and reference who developed procedures and guidelines for the project. Workshops were set up to teach reference staff Dublin Core cataloging basics and pathfinder creation. The reference staff met regularly to create CORC records with guidance and review by cataloging staff. Reference staff is using their subject expertise to create pathfinders in this new medium without needing to learn the intricacies of HTML. Efforts are now underway to export CORC records and pathfinders onto the Library's local Webpac and library Web. It is anticipated that this project will result in a greater number of subject pathfinders available for the end user, increased access to Web resources, and improved collaborative functionality between cataloging and reference staff. *[Article copies available for a fee from The Haworth Document Delivery Service: 1-800-342-9678. E-mail address: <getinfo@haworthpressinc.com> Website: <http://www.HaworthPress.com>]*

KEYWORDS. Reference, cataloging of Internet resources, bibliographic control, CORC, pathfinders, collaboration, cross-training

INTRODUCTION

The question of adequate bibliographic control of Web sites is an issue of fundamental importance that preoccupies librarians, archivists, and scholars. The issue is far from solved. Internet users often are confused, frustrated, and misled by the "chaos" of the Web and the weaknesses of typical search engines. Simple "empowerment" of the users, by giving them unlimited access to the wealth of information on the Web, is not sufficient in itself. Clifford Stoll, author of *Silicon Snake-Oil* and *High Tech Heretic: Why Computers Don't Belong in the Classroom and Other Reflections*, writes, ". . . the Internet is an ocean of unedited data, without any pretense of completeness."[1] No overarching framework of standards and controls has been created to bring order to this virtual world.

Should librarians attempt to superimpose the standards and bibliographic control associated with cataloging onto the Internet? Though Erik Jul notes what he calls the "Three Stoppers" in regard to cataloging Internet resources (there is nothing on the Web worth cataloging; it is too transient; MARC and Anglo-American Cataloging Rules won't work with this kind of material), he rightly concludes that the library that finds and catalogs even one Web source benefits since ". . . the library that systematically integrates the identification, selection, and cataloging of Internet resources into its routine practice will find itself shaping the future."[2]

Cataloging of Internet resources is the key. Michael Gorman stresses that bibliographic control is the "life blood of the library" and that cataloging is a "central activity."[3] Walt Crawford echoes the point by criticizing the idea that cataloging is "passé" and that the "information landscape" of today doesn't allow the luxury of using intellectual efforts to categorize items bibliographically. "Good catalogers" are needed, especially in efforts to bring order into the new world of computer resources.[4] Even Jerry Campbell, who argues that access to collections might better be served by software rather than cataloging, acknowledges that "a good information source is one that includes a librarian" and that we must "convincingly humanize the technological library."[5]

Thus, the "movement to organize the Internet" by librarians is "on a roll" and gaining strength.[6] Since the March 1995 OCLC meeting of library professionals and scholars, who began to discuss what descriptive elements, eventually called the "Dublin Core Metadata Element Set," should be included in cataloging Internet resources, librarians have taken the lead in this effort. In the spring of 1999, the Brown University Library adopted and implemented an innovative approach to the issue of cataloging Internet resources, an approach transcending the traditional division between technical and reference/public services.

BROWN UNIVERSITY LIBRARY AND THE CORC PROJECT–BACKGROUND

The Brown University Library is one of many libraries facing the challenge of evaluating, selecting, and organizing electronic resources available on the Web. Helping our users to access Web resources easily and teaching them the critical thinking skills needed to assess the value of Internet resources relevant to their areas of study and research are two of our priorities. Achieving these objectives, however, requires investment in staff time, allocation of resources, and technical expertise.

The Library has established a long-standing partnership with the bibliographic utility, OCLC, and has participated in InterCat, the first national experiment to catalog electronic resources. In 1999, OCLC launched the Cooperative Online Resource Catalog (CORC) initiative, the purpose of which was to explore the cooperative creation and sharing by libraries of metadata and to produce subject "pathfinders." This came at the time that Brown was discussing better ways to inform users about quality Web sites and how best to create Web-based bibliographies.

Two of the constraints on the traditional cataloging of Internet resources are that it can be labor intensive and costly. It was decided that by joining the CORC project, an efficient and cost-effective way had been found to catalog Web resources. Using the Dublin Core 15 elements as the first step towards the creation of a full MARC record offered the flexibility we were seeking in a cross-functional approach. As Gorman notes, CORC provides a "third way" between the expense of traditional cataloging and the frustration and futility involved in the aimless keyword searching practiced by users.[7]

When the Brown University Library joined the CORC project, representatives from collection development, reference, social sciences data services, cataloging, and serials cataloging met to discuss how Brown would approach the endeavor. Expected outcomes included:

- Identification and selection of no-fee Web resources to supplement the breadth and depth of our existing collections. While the library had been purchasing electronic journals and databases for a number of years, it had not made any provision for incorporating free Web resources that do not require any access restriction, such as a license agreement or password, into the library's collection development policies and procedures.
- Development of subject bibliographies, or "pathfinders," listing both traditional (print) and digital resources for our library Web home page. These would serve as educational tools and guides to our users, and would provide an efficient way to access electronic resources carefully selected for their scope, design, and stability. This would be a primary goal.
- Increasing the pool of staff members who gain experience in the cataloging of electronic resources in a variety of disciplines through exposure to the use of a Web-based catalog, testing the use of automated cataloging tools, and participation in the development of the Dublin Core standard.
- Creating opportunities for staff in technical and public services to collaborate on a project that would foster a better understanding of their operations, and would, by using their complementary skills, support the information needs of our users.

The CORC discussion group soon came to the conclusion that the catalog department alone would not be able to handle the anticipated volume of Internet cataloging. Staff were already juggling a large set of priorities: cataloging currently received print, non-print, and electronic resources, reducing backlogs, addressing retrospective conversion problems, transferring materials to remote storage sites, and processing withdrawals. In addition, they might not necessarily have adequate subject expertise to select those Web sites that would best serve the requirements of our users. A strategy was needed to get appropriate staff involved, especially reference librarians with subject expertise, and then to create a framework for collaboration with catalogers.

The discussion group was well aware of the challenges associated with training reference staff in creating cataloging records. Reference staff could be expected to point out that, because of their other duties, they would not have enough time; that, since the sites were already on the Web, why was there an urgency to have records in the OPAC or to create pathfinders? Could public services staff be expected to understand cataloging rules? Was CORC–new, experimental, and untested–worth a major investment of time and resources? Who would maintain the cataloging records? These reservations were not insignificant or trivial. They needed to be addressed.

IMPLEMENTATION STRATEGY AND TRAINING SCHEDULE

The CORC discussion group decided to introduce the project to the Brown University Library in the following way.

The social sciences reference/collection development librarian and social sciences data services manager volunteered to learn how to search the CORC catalog and to create new records in Dublin Core and subject pathfinders. Statistical and political Web sites (e.g., public opinion, campaign finance, elections) were targeted. These individuals tested the system locally, explored its full potential, and confronted the inevitable bugs and problems. Along with catalogers who understood the system, they took the lead in training other reference specialists.

The trainers demonstrated the CORC system to selectors, provided step by step instruction in the searching of the CORC database and in the construction of bibliographic records, and were available to answer questions and provide advice. This resulted in the elimination of traditional reference ambivalence about cataloging. Trainers also pointed out to selectors the clear benefits that could be gained in the services provided to library users. As Larsgaard notes, "It is ironic that information derived from cataloging had to be called something else–metadata–before noncatalogers dealt with it."[8]

The CORC process does not require time-consuming HTML construction and provides an easy and efficient standardized way of cataloging resources. Pathfinders could include both print and electronic resources, even graphics, that could be exported to the Web version of our catalog (for an example of a Brown CORC pathfinder, go to http://www.brown.edu/Facilities/University_ Library/electronic/Opinion.htm).

Subject specialists and reference librarians began selecting the Web sites to be entered into CORC. Resource discovery tools include, but are not limited to, the weekly *Internet Scout Report*, online *ChoiceReviews*, the *Chronicle of Higher Education*, and electronic academic discussion groups. Using the CORC feature that automatically extracts data from the HTML-coded Web sites and guidelines prepared by the catalog department, participants create a Dublin Core record with a brief description, some personal and corporate name access points, and subject keyword suggestions. Senior level paraprofessionals in the catalog department complete the bibliographic description, assign Library of Congress subject headings and classification numbers, supply additional access points, and provide MARC tagging and coding. Through this collaborative approach, the selector who is most familiar with the electronic resource can choose the data that is most relevant, such as the author, title or alternative title, and subject keyword. Catalog department staff is responsible for ensuring that the record contains all mandatory MARC fields, adheres to the Anglo-American Cataloging Rules, and that all headings are established and verified according to national and local standards. In a final step, CORC records are exported to our online catalog (Innovative Interfaces) and are integrated with other MARC records. The use of the Library of Congress subject headings and authority control assure that users retrieve all types of media that are useful to their teaching and research, in a consistent and efficient manner. Subject specialists and reference librarians design or customize pathfinders in their discipline based on existing sites cataloged in the CORC database. Simplicity and flexibility also characterize the creation of these pathfinders. For example, one can begin a pathfinder by tagging a series of individual records. The CORC software imports the title of each tagged record with the content note, which serves as the description for the resource. The pathfinder can be customized with subsections, additional free text, a banner, and images. Traditional library resources can also be added to the pathfinder and linked to the local Web-based catalog.

To answer the time commitment concerns of selectors, a block of time was set aside for reference staff to work as a group with the trainers. Subject content of pathfinders "in-process" would broaden at this point. To ease concerns about cataloging standards, catalogers would review the new records and pathfinders.

Finally, it was expected that new discipline teams (social sciences, humanities, sciences, history and area studies), incorporating members from both public and technical services, would emphasize as one of their goals an ongoing commitment to the creation of CORC entries and subject pathfinders.

RESULTS

Staff is pleased with the results of the first six months of our combined efforts in enhancing intellectual access to Web resources, in sharing responsibility for some aspects of bibliographic control, and in the collaboration between departments. Both selectors and cataloging staff have expressed enthusiasm for the project. Our involvement with CORC at the local level has provided the impetus for:

- Developing Guidelines for Selection of No-Fee Web Resources (see Table 1). These supplement our Collection Development Policy that was prepared before electronic resources became part of the selection of library materials;
- Creating an intranet request form to catalog no-fee Web resources to serve as a communication tool between selectors and catalogers;
- Developing methods for resource discovery;
- Contributing catalog records to an international endeavor;
- Exposing both cataloging and non-cataloging staff to the challenges of describing, organizing, and integrating Web resources into our collections;
- Creating subject pathfinders for public service staff and library users in an efficient and relatively easy manner;
- Promoting an understanding of shared values and functional collaboration among staff.

This last point is extremely important. For too long, it has been assumed that public and technical services cannot work closely together in a catalog-

TABLE 1. Brown University Library Guidelines for Selection of No-Fee Web Resources for Cataloging in Josiah

The purpose of cataloging no-fee Internet resources is to supplement the breadth and depth of the existing collections and to improve the quality of services available to the University community. Sites chosen for this form of access should meet the following criteria:

Required:
- Be available at no-fee and with no restrictions (no license, registration, passwords, agreements to monitor usage, or printing costs)
- Be authoritative and scholarly (most sites), chosen using common criteria of selection such as scope, content, design, authority, source, reliability, and stability of the site
- Support Brown curricular, research, and/or informational needs
- Not be linked on the Electronic Resources Web as a fully-supported database
- Not require special software on ERD workstations

Preferred:
- Able to be linked directly to the resource at the point where it is most useful
- Have a contact listed for problem reporting by the selector and/or users
- Provide both current and archived information, when possible

Selector Responsibilities:
- Initial recommendations of resources based on selection guidelines
- Regular, ongoing review and evaluation of selected resources for content and organizational changes. The Library has purchased software that will automatically check whether the links on Josiah are still active/accurate
- Deselection of sources when appropriate

ing project because of differing agendas, missions, and skills. The staff at the Brown University Library has shown that it is possible and fruitful for both.

It is equally rewarding to be involved in this innovative and productive collaboration between OCLC and the library community. It is important to have a role in the development of what Terry Noreault, Vice President, OCLC Office of Research, recently described as a "sustainable service that will help keep libraries at the center of the information landscape." The project will undoubtedly result in furthering the development of emerging cataloging standards and knowledge management tools.

NOTES

1. Clifford Stoll, "The Internet? Bah!" *Newsweek* (February 27, 1995): 41.

2. Erik Jul, "Now that We Know the Answer, What are the Questions?" *Journal of Internet Cataloging* 1, no. 3 (1998): 9-14.

3. Michael Gorman, "Metadata or Cataloguing? A False Choice." *Journal of Internet Cataloging* 2, no. 1 (1999): 5-22.

4. Walt Crawford, "The Card Catalog and Other Digital Controversies: What's Obsolete and What's Not In the Age of Information." *American Libraries* 30, no. 1 (January 1999): 52-58.

5. Jerry Campbell, "Building Xanadu: Creating the New Library Paradise." *Collection Management* 22, no. 3/4 (1998): 31-40.

6. Ron Chepesiuk, "Organizing the Internet: The "Core" of the Challenge." *American Libraries* 30, no.1 (January 1999): 60-63.

7. Gorman, p. 13.

8. Holley R. Lange and B. Jean Winkler, "Taming the Internet: Metadata, A Work in Progress." In *Advances in Librarianship*, 21, (1997): 47-72.

CORC and Collaborative Internet Resource Description: A New Partnership for Technical Services, Collection Development and Public Services

Karen Calhoun

SUMMARY. The author describes the "CORC at Cornell" project, undertaken by a small cross-functional team. Using CORC and Dublin Core (DC) as a framework, the team explored a distributed model for Internet resource description, in which catalogers, selectors, and reference specialists participated in producing DC and MARC metadata for the library's OPAC and gateway. After describing the experimental workflow that was developed and tested in the project, the author employs systems analysis techniques to model and discuss the Internet re-

Karen Calhoun is Director, Central Technical Services, Cornell University Library (e-mail: ksc10@cornell.edu).

Author note: First and foremost, I thank the members of the Cornell CORC team, without whose hard work, collaboration, openness, clear insights, advice, patience and good humor, neither our project nor this paper would have happened. They are Martha Hsu (bibliographer at Olin Library), Yumin Jiang (serials cataloger at Mann Library), Jill Powell (reference librarian at the Engineering Library), Don Schnedeker (director of the Management Library), Pam Stansbury (cataloging supervisor in Central Technical Services), and Bill Walters (at the time of this study, a bibliographer at Mann Library). I am also grateful to Ross Atkinson (deputy university librarian) and Janet McCue (director, Mann Library) for their encouragement and support as our CORC project sponsors.

[Haworth co-indexing entry note]: "CORC and Collaborative Internet Resource Description: A New Partnership for Technical Services, Collection Development and Public Services." Calhoun, Karen. Co-published simultaneously in *Journal of Internet Cataloging* (The Haworth Information Press, an imprint of The Haworth Press, Inc.) Vol. 4, No. 1/2, 2001, pp. 131-142; and: *CORC: New Tools and Possibilities for Cooperative Electronic Resource Description* (ed: Karen Calhoun, and John J. Riemer) The Haworth Information Press, an imprint of The Haworth Press, Inc., 2001, pp. 131-142. Single or multiple copies of this article are available for a fee from The Haworth Document Delivery Service [1-800-342-9678, 9:00 a.m. - 5:00 p.m. (EST). E-mail address: getinfo@haworthpressinc.com].

131

source description process. The findings indicate that distributed resource description is both feasible and beneficial, and that staff from various functional areas can readily use DC and CORC. The article concludes with a discussion of issues that warrant further research. *[Article copies available for a fee from The Haworth Document Delivery Service: 1-800-342-9678. E-mail address: <getinfo@haworthpressinc.com> Website: <http://www.HaworthPress.com>]*

KEYWORDS. CORC, electronic resources, Dublin Core metadata, MARC cataloging records, technical services workflow, systems analysis, cross-functional teams, library organization

INTRODUCTION

The Cornell CORC project team attempted to achieve a significant extension of our understanding of Internet resource description and its relationship to library staff roles and practices. For the purpose of this paper, *Internet resource description* is broadly defined to encompass those activities–including conventional cataloging and other types of metadata creation–whose purpose is to create surrogates to facilitate library users' discovery, evaluation, and connection to Internet resources.

At Cornell, as in most libraries, responsibility for resource description generally has been centralized in technical services departments. Because our team experimented with broadly *distributed* resource description, I anticipate that not only cataloging managers and practitioners, but also collection development and reference specialists, will have an interest in our research.

Like many academic research libraries, Cornell's library is seeking innovative, rapid, and cost-effective means to integrate and deliver traditional and digital resources in support of the university's information needs. With its technical and functional framework of Web-accessible shared databases and automated tools, CORC gave our team a full-featured system for experimenting, at low levels of risk and cost, with new standards, procedures, and technologies for resource description. Further–thanks to the metadata interoperability and record export options of CORC–for the first time we had a way to support record creation in Dublin Core (DC) and then integrate the records into our catalog, which can store and index only MARC.

The "CORC at Cornell" project was undertaken by a small, cross-functional research team of seven people. Our research objectives included:

- Comparing record editing/creation in CORC to the procedures and technology now in use for resource description of Web resources;

- Assessing the level, education, and training needed for Web resource description using CORC;
- Exploring the feasibility of a new workflow for creating resource descriptions through collaboration with selectors and/or reference librarians.

CONTEXT OF THE STUDY

At the time the opportunity to participate in CORC arose, Cornell library staff discussions of the best approaches to organizing the library's Web presence–and to organizing ourselves to build, manage, and continually improve that presence–were at a height. In late 1998, we had completed a user study to assess how the Cornell Library Gateway is being used, Gateway users' satisfaction levels, and enhancement needs. The results of the study are reported elsewhere (Koltay and Calhoun 1999). It is worth spending a few moments here, however, to reflect on the implications of that study for library catalogs and gateways of the future. In keeping with the analysis laid out by Ercegovac (1997), the findings of the Cornell Gateway study hint at some fundamental changes in the library environment that, I suggest, demand new operational and organizational assumptions. They are outlined in Table 1.

In a recent campus poll, Cornell seniors ranked the library first among thirty-eight administrative services of the university (Thomas 1999). Clearly, our library operations and organizational structure have been serving the community well. Typically, our principal functional groups (technical services, public services, collection development) have worked independently of one another, with a high degree of autonomy. The chief technical services

TABLE 1. Working Assumptions for Library Information Retrieval Systems

NOW	EMERGING
• Local collection, mostly print	• Many kinds of data sets, local and remote
• Catalog represents the collection but is separate from it	• With full text, catalog and collection are converging
• Highly standardized bibliographic records	• Less structure in indexing, mixed representations of data; metadata can be prescribed by varying rules or be free form
• Centralized responsibility for resource description/metadata creation	• Distributed responsibility for resource description/metadata creation; records come from multiple sources

product–the catalog–has been effective. Overall, the library's driving force has been production–books and journals selected, acquired, cataloged, and shelved; materials circulated; instructional sessions taught; reference questions answered–and staff roles and relationships have been clear.

With the advent of the Internet, however, Cornell library users have many substitutes and complements to the library's products and services. In the crowded information marketplace, the library is experiencing–and responding to–competition and pressure to become more agile, innovative, and user-centered (rather than product- or process-driven). Additional pressure comes from the need to accommodate Internet resources themselves and to integrate them into selection, acquisitions, resource description, and reference work.

Cornell librarians have found that Web-based resources tend to break the mold, operationally and organizationally. An *operational* transition is being driven by the transformation of the catalog away from bibliographic description of a physical collection toward the representation of a virtual repository. Ercegovac notes that "the quest for effective methods to organize diverse virtual collections for the purposes of information retrieval has just begun." Speaking of the *organizational* transition, Duranceau (1998) points to the "identity crisis in serials acquisitions" brought on by the proliferation of Web resources. Going one step further, I speculate that the current winds of change are causing *all* library functional groups to experience defining moments, not only pertaining to their own roles but also with respect to their relationships with other functional groups in the library.

At Cornell, through the Library Gateway, we are striving to build a coherent system for discovery and retrieval from the myriad resources and services available to our library users. In designing our CORC research project, the experience of working on the Gateway, plus the work of Younger (1997) and others noted here, have provided considerable guidance. The Cornell CORC project began in the context of these fundamentals:

1. The *reasons* for resource description have not changed, but the *requirements* have. Creators want their documents to be found, and readers want to find the documents that matter to them;
2. Building a coherent knowledge management system requires the same skills that librarians already have, but evolved beyond their current state. Hill and Intner (1999) treat this subject in detail;
3. Metadata (like money) will continue to make the world go around, because it is the "medium of exchange" for connecting searchers with the information they need.

Hudgins, Agnew, and Brown (1999) underscore the critical importance of metadata for Web resources. Remarking "the central paradox of the Web has proven to be that the more information available on a subject, the greater the likelihood that relevant, authoritative information will not be found," they make a strong case that metadata for Internet resources has never been more important than now.

EXPERIMENTAL WORKFLOW

To gather insights into the research questions, the CORC team developed an experimental workflow to be used by team members. We also analyzed the existing production workflow for producing Internet resource descriptions. (Note: Selecting, acquiring, and describing print resources is nearly always a linear process in which one person works independently on each step. As can be seen from the workflow description that follows, selecting, "acquiring," and describing Internet resources, by contrast, is an iterative, looping process that can involve many individuals.)

The *existing* Cornell workflow usually includes the following steps:

Steps

1. A selector* identifies and selects an Internet resource;
2. The selector initiates a request to acquire and/or catalog the resource (generally using the "Networked Resource Selection Form" at http://www.library.cornell.edu/tsmanual/EdocsFORM.html);
3. Acquisitions staff and the selector exchange inquiries as needed;
4. Acquisitions staff negotiate with vendor/publisher/author (for licensed resources);
5. Acquisitions staff prepare preliminary data for a resource description (MARC format) and forward the selection form to cataloging;**
6. Acquisitions/catalogers/selectors exchange inquiries as needed;
7. Catalogers consult the resource, cataloging standards and databases to revise and complete the preliminary data for the resource description;
8. Catalogers/acquisitions/selectors/information technology staff exchange inquiries as needed;
9. The cataloger produces the resource description for our NOTIS catalog and the Library Gateway.

*For resources that are very expensive and/or multidisciplinary, a standing committee makes selection decisions. For resources that are particularly troublesome from a policy or processing point of view, another standing committee intervenes.

**Except in the case of aggregations that contain many full-text journals, we are beginning to experiment with obtaining a set of records for the titles in the aggregation, and processing them as a batch.

The *experimental* workflow we developed and tested in the CORC project was similar to the existing workflow, except that: (a) selectors prepare the preliminary records in CORC, using the DC standard and (b) reference librarians as well as selectors identify, choose, and create preliminary records for Internet resources. Later, catalogers use CORC to finish the records in MARC format, then export the metadata to the NOTIS catalog and thence to our Library Gateway. In our research project, to keep the scope of our project manageable, we dealt with unlicensed resources only.

The DC elements, with their readily understood names and labels, were designed for flexibility and ease of use by those without traditional cataloging expertise (for more information, visit http://purl.oclc.org/docs/core/index. html). Indeed, the DC's initial purpose was author-generated description of Web resources capable of producing consistent, helpful indexing. In CORC, the DC elements are mapped to MARC record elements (or vice versa) for conversion and export. The mapping supports the interoperability of DC and MARC records in the CORC database.

The design of our experimental workflow has, at its heart, the recognition that the Internet resource description process can be dynamic–that is, initially, the content of a record can be quite minimal, but depending on library policy and practice, it can be modified and enriched over time.

SYSTEMS ANALYSIS

Conceptualizing the Internet resource description process can be difficult. Flowcharting is linear and most suited to the description of closed systems (that is, processes that exist independently, that are complete unto themselves). As demonstrated by Richardson (1999) in his modeling of the reference transaction, an alternative to flowcharting is systems analysis. Its graphic representation of inputs and outputs offers a top-down perspective that can lead to new insights. The following section of this paper is an adaptation of Richardson's systems analysis approach; it attempts to model our experimental Internet resource description process as a system.

Systems have users and a primary goal. The users of our experimental Internet resource description system were selectors, acquisitions and cataloging staff, other library staff, and readers. The system's primary goal was to create a "medium of exchange" (metadata) to connect readers with relevant Internet resources through our catalog and Gateway.

Figure 1 is a simplified graphical representation of the context of our experimental resource description system. It is an illustrative rather than comprehensive depiction of the process we followed in our CORC project. Solid lines designate the flows of data in the system. The dotted line flows designate inquiries and responses exchanged among library staff in the

FIGURE 1. Context of the Experimental Internet Resource Description System

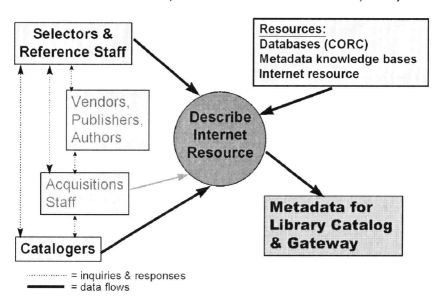

course of producing resource descriptions. In a production system, selectors and acquisitions staff would have exchanged inquiries and responses with vendors, publishers, and/or authors as well; thus, I've included grayed-out boxes in the figure as placeholders (since in our CORC project, we dealt with unlicensed resources only).

Because, in our experimental system, resource description was broadly distributed, rather than centralized in technical services, data flowed in from numerous sources: selectors, reference staff, and catalogers. (In a production workflow, data would also have come from acquisitions; thus I've included acquisitions in the diagram.)

Data also flowed in from resource description databases (in this case CORC), from metadata knowledge bases (either DC or MARC/AACR2), and from the Internet resources themselves. Our resource description process ended with the output of metadata records and their integration into the catalog and Library Gateway.

Systems also have requirements (indicating what they are intended to do) and constraints. In our experimental system, the requirements were that descriptions must be created for all requests entering the CORC workflow (within the limits we set on the project scope), and that the completed record must conform to current Cornell cataloging standards for e-resources. (As will be discussed subsequently, a more suitable requirement would have been that the resource descriptions be "useful"–that is, meet readers' needs–assuming we could define "useful.")

One system constraint was that resource descriptions must be produced in a timely and cost-effective manner. Another had to do with the collaborative nature of the Internet resource description process: the system must facilitate, and not impede, communication between functional groups. Further, it must allow ready access to up-to-date metadata knowledge bases and appropriate resource description tools.

RESULTS AND DISCUSSION

Our experience in the CORC project suggests that the changes we tested to the workflow can ease and streamline the production of Internet resource descriptions. It also suggests that distributed resource description is both feasible and beneficial, and that selectors and reference librarians can readily use DC to create preliminary records using CORC. CORC enables us to spread the wealth (of resource description) outside the technical services units. Our results suggest that the skills required to use CORC are basic familiarity with computers and the ability to move around in, and manipulate, online forms and records. Without having to be a cataloging specialist, a library staff member has the opportunity to create an online description, with an annotation and keywords to make it findable in our catalog. The cataloger uses the information and converts it to MARC, improving efficiency and accuracy.

Selectors on the team welcomed not having to use the paper- or e-mail-based Networked Resource Selection Form, instead recording the information directly in the DC record. Another major plus was finding records already in CORC for most of the resources that were selected during the project. Catalogers on the team were delighted to have a preliminary record to start with; in particular, it saved their time to have the selector or reference librarian prepare an annotation or summary note (MARC 520 field) on the resource (Cornell policy requires a 520 field for all networked resource titles). Being able to flip back and forth between DC and MARC views of a record was the keystone of our workflow. Along the same lines, the team agreed that the most productive conversations about DC and MARC will assume that both have their place at Cornell. We should focus on how to forge a complementary relationship between the two standards, striving to optimize the strengths of each.

As hoped, the systems analysis of our experimental workflow has facilitated an extension of our understanding of Internet resource description and its relationship to staff roles and interactions. Using this methodology allowed us to visualize the process and more fully comprehend the potential benefits of a distributed resource description system for Internet resources.

Figure 2 builds in some additional possibilities to the system depicted previously in this paper (to make the figure easier to read, the dotted lines designating communication between groups have been removed). In this new context, the responsibility for producing resource descriptions is even more widely distributed. Metadata can flow from information technology staff, as was illustrated at the University of Tennessee-Knoxville (Britten et al. 2000) when library systems staff programmatically developed a set of brief records for the titles embedded in Lexis/Nexis' Academic Universe. Metadata can also flow from vendors, publishers, and authors themselves, as was the case when EBSCO made a record set available for the full text titles in its Academic Search Elite aggregation (PCC Task Group 2000).

Figure 2 depicts a resource description system that could be very effective for making Internet resource descriptions available more quickly, in greater numbers, and at less cost, assuming it is capable of delivering records that are useful to readers. However, I anticipate many obstacles to the full deployment of such a system. I believe the obstacles will not be technical or operational, but organizational and attitudinal. At Cornell, at least, many of us are deeply vested in existing processes and organizational structures. Not only that, the existing processes and structures still function well for most items

FIGURE 2. Context of a Widely Distributed Internet Resource Decription System

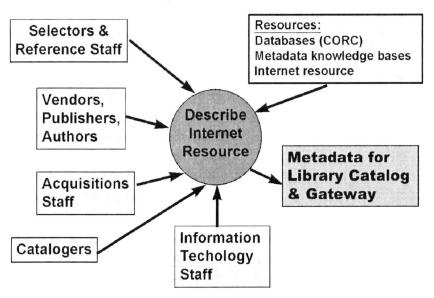

that are added to the collections. Finally, because we are and will be in a transitional state for some time, staff must strike an appropriate balance between their everyday work and new ways of doing things.

In conclusion, our experiences in the CORC project have led to a number of recommendations for our Cornell colleagues and the library administration. Some of the recommendations, which we discussed at a library-wide meeting in early 2000, are briefly summarized below:

1. Library staff should have the option to use CORC to precatalog Internet resources, using DC, and for other purposes;
2. Members of the CORC team should coordinate the preparation of brief guidelines for the use of DC in our library;
3. Reference librarians should have broader roles in the selection of Internet resources;
4. CORC training sessions should become a regular part of the Cornell library staff training program.

The "CORC at Cornell" final report (Calhoun et al. 1999) presents the recommendations in detail.

ISSUES FOR FURTHER INVESTIGATION

As might be expected, as we worked on each of our research objectives, we turned up at least as many questions as answers. The following list, drawn from team meeting notes and e-mails, summarizes some of the issues we discussed.

- Who should select Internet resources for the collection? How can the library take better advantage of what reference staff know about Internet resources and use that knowledge in the selection process? Many reference staff do selection now, but should the opportunity be opened to all? We believe that it is both beneficial and practical for reference staff to broaden their role. At the same time, selectors have an important role to play in vetting selections and maintaining control of what is selected. How can we achieve the best of both worlds?
- How can we effectively store, retrieve, and share evaluative (e.g., reviews, selector decisions) and managerial (e.g., licensing, fund codes, troubleshooting) metadata of importance to selectors and acquisitions staff? Neither MARC nor DC records are adequate for storing this kind of information. In any case, it is probably not appropriate to store this kind of information in shared CORC database records. How might Cornell build the systematic collection and online storage of this kind of metadata into the workflow? What sorts of information should be stored? The team's final report includes some preliminary work on these questions.

- To be effective, especially for those unaccustomed to creating resource descriptions, working in CORC must be quick and convenient. Editing, such as adjusting subject headings and fields in the record, must not be cumbersome. In general, the CORC automated tools, such as the harvester, are great time savers. We eagerly anticipate the arrival of a CORC enhancement to reduce the number of bad URLs and duplicate records now in the database. Our final report includes a number of detailed suggestions for OCLC.
- If the creation of Internet resource descriptions is distributed at Cornell, how much will be expected of those creating preliminary records? How should we implement the DC element set? There should be guidelines, but they must be simple and straightforward to teach and use. We don't want using DC to be tedious, time-consuming or complicated. We found the work of the CORC participants at the University of Minnesota (Hearn 1999) helpful in this regard.
- How much is enough in a record for an Internet resource when the object itself is one click away from the metadata? How useful are all the different elements in our present resource descriptions to our readers? What level(s) of cataloging are appropriate, in which circumstances? While we agreed that even a skeletal DC record enables better indexing and retrieval, we found the present heterogeneous mixture of DC practices encoded in CORC records less than optimal. The key question to answer is: *What is useful to readers?* In team meetings, we returned several times to an article by Lundgren and Simpson (1999), who studied reader preference for particular metadata elements at the University of Florida. Their study attempts to provide a framework for determining the most-desired elements in an Internet resource description, based on a survey of graduate students. The most highly-rated elements were title, primary author or creator, Internet address (URL), and summary note or abstract. Our team gained Lundgren and Simpson's permission to use their survey instrument in our own study. To date, we have completed only a pretest of the survey with members of our library advisory boards, but we feel that further efforts to carry out the survey at Cornell would yield information that is critically needed to guide our decision-making about record content.

REFERENCES CITED

Britten, William A. et al. 2000. Access to periodicals holdings information: creating links between databases and the library catalog. *Library collections, acquisitions, and technical services* (forthcoming).

Calhoun, Karen et al. 1999. CORC at Cornell project: final report. Available at: http://campusgw.library.cornell.edu/corc/corc-final.htm. Accessed: December 23, 1999.

Duranceau, Ellen Finnie. 1998. Beyond print: revisioning serials acquisitions for the digital age. *Serials librarian* 33, no. 1-2: 83-106. Available: http://web.mit.edu/waynej/www/duranceau.htm. Accessed: December 23, 1999.

Ercegovac, Zorana. 1997. The interpretations of library use in the age of digital libraries: virtualizing the name. *Library & information science research* 19, no. 1: 35-51.

Hearn, Steven. 1999. Content standard for CORC Dublin Core records-Rev. 1999-05-25 (University of Minnesota). Available: http://www.lib.umn.edu/ts/drafts/Cat/CORC/contstand.html. Accessed: September 28, 1999.

Hill, Janet Swan, and Sheila S. Intner. 1999. Preparing for a cataloging career: from cataloging to knowledge management. An invited paper for the ALA Congress on Professional Education, Washington, DC, April 30-May 1, 1999. Available: http://www.ala.org/congress/hill-intner_print.html. Accessed: December 23, 1999.

Hudgins, Jean, Grace Agnew, and Elizabeth Brown. 1999. *Getting mileage out of metadata: applications for the library.* Chicago: American Library Association.

Koltay, Zsuzsa, and Karen Calhoun. 1999. Designing for Wow! The optimal information gateway. In *Racing toward tomorrow: proceedings of the ninth national conference of the Association of College and Research Libraries* (Chicago: American Library Association, 1999), 154-60. Available (requires Adobe Acrobat): http://www.ala.org/acrl/koltay.pdf. Accessed: December 23, 1999.

Lundgren, Jimmie, and Betsy Simpson. 1999. Looking through users' eyes: what do graduate students need to know about Internet resources via the library catalog? *Journal of Internet cataloging* 1, no. 4: 31-44.

Program for Cooperative Cataloging (PCC). Standing Committee on Automation (SCA). Task Group on Journals in Aggregator Databases. 2000. Final report. Available: http://lcweb.loc.gov/catdir/pcc/aggfinal.html. Accessed: March 11, 2000.

Richardson, John V. Jr. 1999. Understanding the reference transaction: a systems analysis perspective. *College & research libraries* 60, no. 3: 211-22.

Thomas, Sarah E. 1999. Cornell University Library Annual Report, 1998-1999. Available at: http://www.library.cornell.edu/ulib/report98-99.html. Accessed: March 9, 2000.

Younger, Jennifer A. 1997. Resources description in the digital age. *Library trends* 45, no. 3: 462-81.

Dublin Core and Serials

Wayne Jones

SUMMARY. The article examines the adequacy of the Dublin Core element set (version 1.1) for describing serials and finds that, overall, it works well, except for dates and the volume/date designation. *[Article copies available for a fee from The Haworth Document Delivery Service: 1-800-342-9678. E-mail address: <getinfo@haworthpressinc.com> Website: <http://www.HaworthPress.com>]*

KEYWORDS. Serials, e-serials, Dublin Core, cataloging, metadata, CORC

INTRODUCTION

I turned 40 last year and so gained the right to reminisce about my professional past as a compensation for my declining physical and mental abilities. Please bear with me. When I first started as a serials cataloger, there were no Internet and no e-serials, at least none that we were cataloging. We did our bibliographic records directly online in an old (but functional) character-based system, but used manual typewriters to clack out our authoritative records on worksheets that were magically entered into the system by input clerks at the other end of the room. We had some luxuries though. Every time I cataloged a serial that continued another, I retrospectively examined its entire bibliographic history from volume 1, number 1, to date and made any necessary adjustments in the records. It was a very labor-intensive policy for cataloging serials,

Wayne Jones is Head of Serials Cataloging at MIT and Associate Editor of *The Serials Librari*an (e-mail: waynej@mit.edu).

[Haworth co-indexing entry note]: "Dublin Core and Serials." Jones, Wayne. Co-published simultaneously in *Journal of Internet Cataloging* (The Haworth Information Press, an imprint of The Haworth Press, Inc.) Vol. 4, No. 1/2, 2001, pp. 143-148; and: *CORC: New Tools and Possibilities for Cooperative Electronic Resource Description* (ed: Karen Calhoun, and John J. Riemer) The Haworth Information Press, an imprint of The Haworth Press, Inc., 2001, pp. 143-148. Single or multiple copies of this article are available for a fee from The Haworth Document Delivery Service [1-800-342-9678, 9:00 a.m. - 5:00 p.m. (EST). E-mail address: getinfo@haworthpressinc.com].

but it certainly did have the side effect of keeping the database up to date, and training a new librarian in the intricacies of serials and relationships.

A policy like that seems laughably impossible these days. There is too much to catalog, both in hard copy and online, and a large part of the bibliographic effort is toward shortening the record, determining what parts of it patrons use and don't use, and not wasting time by including and maintaining the latter. The core record is the standard, and the full record is the exception.[1]

This may or may not be a positive development in bibliographic control, but it is the context in which any discussion of serials cataloging takes place. The Dublin Core (DC) was developed in this environment, in which the dominant metaphor used to suggest the proportions of the information situation is "explosion." There are too many items or sites or "knowledge objects"[2] or *things* to control bibliographically, and so, if there is any hope of gaining that control over a reasonably sized subset of them, then the philosophy of the cataloging scheme should be simple and basic. A DC record–in fact any cataloging record these days–should be relatively easy to create and to interpret and should provide the fundamental access that the user needs. The balance between fulsome description and spare access must be carefully considered, like furnishing a room: a severely minimalist décor may not provide the basic necessities and comforts you have come to expect, whereas a place cluttered with objects may take a lot of effort to create and make it hard for you to get around in anyway.

THE ESSENTIALS IN A SERIAL RECORD

It is unfair to dismiss Dublin Core because it does not do all of what MARC does. MARC has had thirty-five years of development to DC's five, and the circumstances and purposes of the development are not identical. The real question is: *What aspects of a serial have to be recorded in order for the resulting record to be considered complete and useful?*

Most of these are obvious–titles, volume/date designation, publishing information, relationships, notes, names–and overall the fifteen elements of the Dublin Core accommodate the description of serials very well. What follows is a discussion of a couple of details which could be instituted in Dublin Core in order to improve description and access for serials.

WHAT DUBLIN CORE DOESN'T ACCOMMODATE WELL

The main aspects of a serial which DC doesn't accommodate well are volume/date designation and dates.

Volume/Date Designation

MARC 362

This is one of the key fields necessary in the bibliographic identification of serials, but there is no provision for it in Dublin Core. It typically contains a numeric and/or alphabetic designation, and/or a date indicating coverage, and is often more relevant than the simple publishing information. For example, it is more important for the user to know that an annual report covers 1999/2000 than to know that it was published in 1999 or to know that a forecasting report covers 2000/2005 than to know that it was in fact published in 1998. And the designation "Vol. 1, no. 1" is generally all the reassurance a user needs to know that he or she need not search out any issues of the journal before *that* one.

There are Coverage and Date elements in Dublin Core, but neither of them seems to be designed or used for recording the volume/date designation. The Coverage element has potential, however. It is designed to be used to record

> [t]he extent or scope of the content of the resource . . . Coverage will typically include spatial location (a place name or geographic coordinates), temporal period (a period label, date, or date range) or jurisdiction (such as a named administrative entity). Recommended best practice is to select a value from a controlled vocabulary (for example, the [Getty] Thesaurus of Geographic Names [TGN]) and that, where appropriate, named places or time periods be used in preference to numeric identifiers such as sets of coordinates or date ranges.[3]

An argument could be made that the volume/date designation falls into the category of "extent or scope of the content of the resource" or perhaps even "temporal period," but that is not the way the DC element is used or apparently intended. In the Library of Congress's mapping between Dublin Core and MARC, the Coverage element maps to several MARC fields (500, 522, and 513) but not to 362.[4] And in the CORC database, records which have a 362 field in a MARC view do not display the information in that field at all in a Dublin Core view.[5]

The Date element is likewise not used for the volume/date designation, and, in fact, it would be less appropriate. Even though the criteria for including information in this element are promisingly general–"[a] date associated with an event in the life cycle of the resource"[6]–it is limited to chronological data, and numeric or alphabetic designations would be inappropriate or extraneous.[7]

Dates

MARC 008, 260, 362

The basic date recorded in a Dublin Core record is one in the form YYYY-MM-DD, in accordance with ISO standard 8601 1988(E)[8] and the so-called W3C "note" or profile which limits the valid date formats.[9] (This note was adopted at the 7th Dublin Core Metadata Workshop in Frankfurt in October 1999.[10]) As mentioned above, the date of a resource, as recorded in the Date element, is defined so broadly that it could legitimately be used for the resource's date of first publication, last update, date of an event described in the resource, or several other types of date. Hence the wide variety of MARC fields to which this element maps.[11]

The difficulty with the Dublin Core Date element, as applied to a serial, is that the result may be ambiguous. For example, in CORC (as it existed December 1999) the Date element, for serials and non-serials, is generated from character positions 07-10 (date 1) and 11-14 (date 2) of the 008, and displays in the Dublin Core view as a qualified element with the label "Date.Issued." Some typical examples are:

Date.Issued   1998-9999 (a journal);[12]
Date.Issued   1995-9999 (a Website; simple date 1 and date 2 in 008);[13]
Date.Issued   1999-12-01 (a Website; year in date 1, month and day in date 2, and value "e" for detailed date in type of date code);[14]
Date.Issued   199-9999 (a Website with value "u" as the 4th character in date 1);[15]
Date.Issued   199 (a Website with value "u" as the 4th character in date 1 and value "s" for single date in type of date code).[16]

The ambiguity is not the result of the Dublin Core or the CORC folks fiddling with the ISO date standard for their own "local" purposes–apart from the use of the hyphen to represent date ranges, all those dates above are compliant with ISO 8601–but rather from some bad basic accepted practices which are built into the standard itself: truncating some of the elements in a recorded date; use of the forward slash ("/") to indicate a range of dates; and, most germane to Dublin Core and the examples cited above, the omission of a digit from a date in order to indicate an unknown part.

The first two of these may be dealt with briefly. The W3C profile of the ISO standard specifically disallows the practice of abbreviating a year to two digits:

> A particular problem with ISO 8601 is that it allows the century to be omitted from years, which is likely to cause trouble as we approach the year 2000. This profile avoids the problem by expressing the year as four digits in all cases.[17]

As for the use of the slash, a solution to the "range problem" was suggested at the 7th Dublin Core Metadata Workshop: instead of indicating a range within a single Date element, define qualifiers so that the first date in the range is recorded in one Date element, and the second date is recorded in another.[18]

Creators and users of records based on that good ole metadata standard called MARC are accustomed to a single fixed-field date which is always comprised of four characters. In MARC, when a precise digit in any part of that date is unknown, the letter "u" is recorded. That does not have to be the specific practice which is adopted in Dublin Core, but a tweaking of the ISO standard to prescribe a four-character date in all cases for a single year would serve users of DC records very well (at least until the year 10,000). And it would be consistent with the W3C profile's recommendation that the first two digits of a year not be omitted as the truncation in the ISO standard allows.

CONCLUSIONS AND RECOMMENDATIONS

Any perceived shortcomings of the Dublin Core element set are not eliminated simply by adding more elements or by declaring the whole thing inadequate and starting over with something else or reverting to MARC–even if that were possible. The philosophy of Dublin Core, partly born of necessity and partly of a practical strategy to encourage and enable more users to create more metadata, is solid: define only as many data elements as are *absolutely essential* for providing access to the wealth of resources that are out there. There are enough DC elements already, and any finessing may be accomplished by other means. Specifically, for the data elements discussed in this article, my recommendations are:

- define a qualifier to the Coverage element for the volume/date designation;
- prescribe a four-digit date in all cases for a single year, with unknown digits indicated by a "u" or some other method.

These are relatively minor modifications. The Dublin Core elements do indeed generally accommodate serials pretty well, and so it is only the details that have to be worked out now.

NOTES

1. For a description of the rationale and the details of the core record, see the *CONSER Editing Guide*, section B6, or the CONSER Website at http://lcweb. loc.gov/acq/conser/recordreq.html.

2. During his address on Nov. 3, 1999, to attendees of the second CORC Participants Meeting in Dublin, OH, OCLC President and CEO Jay Jordan used the term "knowledge objects" to refer to resources that might be cataloged in CORC.

3. *Dublin Core Metadata Element Set: Reference Description*, version 1.1, "Coverage," http://purl.org/DC/documents/rec-dces-19990702.htm.

4. *Dublin Core/MARC/GILS Crosswalk*, http://lcweb.loc.gov/marc/dccross.html.

5. To see examples, search the title keyword "journal" in the CORC catalog at http://corc.oclc.org/, and switch back and forth between the various MARC and DC views.

6. *Dublin Core Metadata Element Set*, "Date," http://purl.org/DC/documents/rec-dces-19990702.htm.

7. The volume/date designation (or, more accurately, the "numeric and/or alphabetic, chronological, or other designation") is the element recorded in area 3 for serials according to the *Anglo-American Cataloguing Rules*. There are three other types of resources for which area 3 may be routinely applicable: cartographic materials ("mathematical data," MARC 255), music ("musical presentation statement," MARC 254), and computer files ("file characteristics," MARC 256). None of these MARC fields is specifically mapped to from Dublin Core, though at the risk of betraying an unintentional serials bias on my part, I think that the information recorded in a *serials* area 3 is less relegatable to some other element in DC than the other area 3's. For details about area 3, see the .3 rules in chapters 3, 5, 9, and 12 of *AACR*, 2nd ed., 1988 rev. (Chicago: American Library Association, 1988).

8. International Organization for Standardization, *Data Elements and Interchange Formats*: *Information Interchange*: *Representation of Dates and Times: ISO 8601:1988/Cor.1:1991(E)*, 1st ed. (Geneva: ISO, 1991), http://www.iso.ch/markete/8601.pdf.

9. W3C, *Date and Time Formats*: *Note-Datetime* (Sept. 15, 1997), http://www.w3.org/TR/NOTE-datetime.

10. 7th Dublin Core Metadata Workshop, *Results of the Working Groups*, Oct. 25-27, "DC Date and Coverage WG," slide 4, http://www.ddb.de/partner/dc7conference/results/dc7-date-coverage/sld004.htm.

11. *Dublin Core Metadata Element Set*, "Date," http://purl.org/DC/documents/rec-dces-19990702.htm.

12. Record for *Journal of Neural Transmission*, CORC record number 186364 (all CORC records viewed Dec. 4, 1999).

13. Record for "The World Wide Web Acronym and Abbreviation Server," CORC record number 33894.

14. Record for "The Planetary Society," CORC record number 42287.

15. Record for "AIAA, American Institute of Aeronautics and Astronautics," CORC record number 52844.

16. Record for "Cyburbia.org," CORC record number 109254.

17. W3C, http://www.w3.org/TR/NOTE-datetime.

18. 7th Dublin Core Metadata Workshop, http://www.ddb.de/partner/dc7conference/results/dc7-date-coverage/sld004.htm.

Using the Dublin Core
to Document Digital Art:
A Case Study

Ann Hanlon
Ann Copeland

SUMMARY. The @art gallery is a digital art gallery affiliated with the University of Illinois at Urbana-Champaign School of Art and Design. The exhibits in the gallery consist entirely of digital art often created exclusively for the Web environment. The authors, as part of a project conducted for the Digital Imaging and Media Technology Initiative at the University of Illinois, used the gallery for a case study to test the applicability of the Dublin Core metadata format for digital art. In addition, they used the Arts and Humanities Data Service's *Discovering Online Resources Across the Humanities* as a guide to best practice. Several challenges were presented by this study, including how best to extend Dublin Core to accommodate the multiple access points necessary to discover a work of digital art, how best to encode the FORMAT element to effectively describe the tools needed to view works of digital art, and whether their use of Dublin Core would translate into a record

Ann Hanlon is a graduate assistant, University of Illinois Digital Imaging and Media Technology Initiative (e-mail: a-hanlon@alexia.lis.uiuc.edu).

Ann Copeland is Serials Team Leader, University of Illinois Library (e-mail: awcopela@uiuc.edu).

The authors thank Beth Sandore, Head, University of Illinois Digital Imaging and Media Technology Initiative (e-mail: sandore@uiuc.edu), and Alex Dunkel, a Consultant/Network Analyst, University of Illinois Computing and Communications Services Office (e-mail: dunkel@ntx1.cso.uiuc.edu), for their contributions to this article.

[Haworth co-indexing entry note]: "Using the Dublin Core to Document Digital Art: A Case Study." Hanlon, Ann, and Ann Copeland. Co-published simultaneously in *Journal of Internet Cataloging* (The Haworth Information Press, an imprint of The Haworth Press, Inc.) Vol. 4, No. 1/2, 2001, pp. 149-161; and: *CORC: New Tools and Possibilities for Cooperative Electronic Resource Description* (ed: Karen Calhoun, and John J. Riemer) The Haworth Information Press, an imprint of The Haworth Press, Inc., 2001, pp. 149-161. Single or multiple copies of this article are available for a fee from The Haworth Document Delivery Service [1-800-342-9678, 9:00 a.m. - 5:00 p.m. (EST). E-mail address: getinfo@haworthpressinc.com].

in CORC. The study indicates that Dublin Core elements must be qualified and repeated to clearly document the particular and unique characteristics of digital art and that the Dublin Core implementation in CORC does not always accommodate this use of Dublin Core. *[Article copies available for a fee from The Haworth Document Delivery Service: 1-800-342-9678. E-mail address: <getinfo@haworthpressinc.com> Website: <http://www.HaworthPress.com>]*

KEYWORDS. Digital art, visual art, metadata, Dublin Core, CORC, image retrieval

INTRODUCTION

The *@art gallery*[1] is an online gallery of digital art curated by Joseph Squier and Nan Goggin, who are both faculty at the University of Illinois School of Art and Design. The gallery showcases work created specifically for an electronic environment. The works residing in the *@art gallery* are not reproductions derived from "originals" (unlike, say, the images found in online image databases such as MESL or AMICO, or historical collections databases such as the Library of Congress American Memory Collections). They are the originals–inasmuch as that concept carries over into an electronic environment.

Describing and documenting such digitally conceived art, which has no surrogate or corresponding physical manifestation, fell within the purview of the Digital Imaging and Media Technology Initiative (DIMTI),[2] a unit of the University of Illinois Library. The DIMTI was established in 1994 to explore the use of multimedia and network technology in order to promote widespread digital access to the Library's unique collections. The DIMTI Head, Beth Sandore, and the authors decided to test the boundaries of the Dublin Core metadata format as implemented in CORC.[3] We asked: could Dublin Core accommodate the demanding requirements of the digital art format represented by the *@art gallery* archives?

We began by looking at the particular challenges presented by the *@art gallery* in the areas of retrieval and documentation and asked some key questions of the Dublin Core format:

1. Is Dublin Core adequate for describing the exhibits in the *@art gallery* archives? How does it handle the complex access points that are required?
2. Can Dublin Core adequately represent the dynamic relationships between pieces, exhibits, and the gallery as a whole?

3. Can Dublin Core elements adequately document the tools needed to access and activate digital art?
4. How do Dublin Core and CORC deal with subject analysis for conceptual works of art?

We first worked with Dublin Core in theory, using guidelines from the Arts and Humanities Data Service's *Discovering Online Resources Across the Humanities: a Practical Implementation of the Dublin Core.*[4] We chose these guidelines because they offered a useful mix of arts and humanities projects from which to draw examples. In addition to visual arts, these guidelines included examples and best practice for the performing arts and electronic texts. These provided needed additional context for the *@art gallery* archives as the works incorporate texts and narratives in addition to their visual components. We also considered Dublin Core's current configuration in OCLC's CORC project.

IS DUBLIN CORE ADEQUATE FOR DESCRIBING THE EXHIBITS IN THE @ART GALLERY ARCHIVES? HOW DOES IT HANDLE THE COMPLEX ACCESS POINTS THAT ARE REQUIRED?

Tools such as the Dublin Core are intended in part to make access to non-book material possible in an environment similar to that traditionally used to search for textual materials (such as an OPAC). Cataloging digital media-as well as other formats not normally included in the OPAC, such as archival finding aids, or museum objects, makes it possible for the user to discover diverse formats with a unifying element that is (ideally) relevant to his or her project. The discovery of diverse formats in a routine search can also introduce a user to the potential of non-print resources they had not previously contemplated. OCLC's CORC project, by facilitating the cataloging of digital resources, should greatly enhance such resource discovery.

The *@art gallery* is an excellent example of a resource that typically might be under-utilized outside its primary context as original, interactive, contemporary art. Because the works of art contained in the gallery address a broad spectrum of social, aesthetic and political subjects, the challenge for Dublin Core (and, indeed, any other cataloging format, such as MARC) is to adequately represent the critical, satirical, and subtle nuances of the artworks, while providing sufficient access points for their retrieval.

For example, an art series such as Michael Ensdorf's "Minor Players" uses images taken from well-documented historical events and "investigate[s] the collective non-identity of mostly anonymous individuals depicted in the digitized media imagery" (Ensdorf, "Minor Players Series").[5] (See Figure 1.) Ensdorf's visual investigation intersects with a wide range of

FIGURE 1

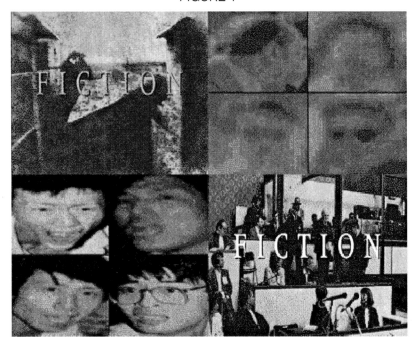

Michael Ensdorf, "Minor Players Series." From *Art as Signal: Parts of the Loop.*

disciplines, including journalism, communications, history, and graphic design. For a history student looking for a new perspective on the events depicted or a journalism student interested in alternative commentary on the media, Ensdorf's art opens up a whole new body of work from which to draw new points of view and on which to construct original research.

As Ensdorf's work illustrates, the co-existence of digital art with traditional texts in an OPAC is essential to making this new art form accessible beyond the art world. But their retrieval is impossible using the keyword searching prevalent on the Web. Their best chance for wide accessibility is through cataloging and the analysis of access points that is integral to that activity. To that end, it is of paramount concern that proposed metadata formats like Dublin Core are able to incorporate the key characteristics of digital art works in such a manner that generalizes their content so that it can coexist with other formats while providing information about their specific and unique characteristics.

We hoped to accomplish this goal by stretching the repeatability and extensibility of Dublin Core's fifteen elements to accommodate the *@art* *gallery*. We began with the CREATOR field and tested its ability to accommodate the idiosyncrasies of the works in the @*art gallery* archives. We first considered the exhibit, *The Lot Project: contributing to mobility*, which lists nine participating artists, two of whom are corporate entities with important geographic locations. Extending Dublin Core beyond its "Simple" stage is a necessity if a user is to make sense of all those names; likewise, to leave out even one is to subtract a key access point. Therefore, following examples from the Arts and Humanities Data Service's *Discovering Online Resources Across the Humanities*, we repeated the CREATOR field nine times, each time with a matching extension of the CREATOR field called CREATOR.*role*, to distinguish between corporate names and personal names. Further extending the CREATOR field, we included a sub-element field for the geographic location of corporate groups, with the guidance of Rebecca Guenther's 1997 document, *Dublin Core Qualifiers/Substructure* (Figure 2).[6]

Our rationale for an extended CREATOR entry concerns the cooperative nature of an exhibit like *The Lot Project: contributing to mobility*, as well as our decision to create records at the exhibit rather than individual piece level. Some aspects of the *The Lot Project* may be attributable to a single creator; however, the totality of the exhibit and the important access points for the exhibit call for a complete record of all the primarily contributing parties.

As *The Lot Project* record shows, the extensibility of the Dublin Core fields proved crucial to us in cataloging the @*art gallery* archives. Without the ability to document in what specific way the CREATOR field or the DATE or PUBLISHER field is being used, and perhaps, even, whose best practice manual was being used to extend them, the Dublin Core is inadequate. By piecing out individual access points and connecting groups of distinct entries through a numbering scheme, the extended Dublin Core record provides descriptive access points that delineate individual roles among a complex group of creators.

In his April 1999 report on the "State of the Dublin Core Metadata Initiative," Stuart Weibel acknowledged the need for "Identifying a formal encoding standard" to make "otherwise ambiguous value[s] useful" and for the specification of a formal substructure, such as a scheme qualifier, to indicate compound values in an element.[7] In the case of *The Lot Project*, this would mean that the geographic location of corporate authors, as well as CREATOR roles, would be specified in an extended Dublin Core scheme, perhaps similar to our own. We feel that it is precisely this kind of specificity that is necessary to make Dublin Core useful for discovering digital art exhibits and look forward to improvement and agreement on the nature of that structure.

We found it troubling that the CORC implementation of Dublin Core severely limits extensions. Because the extensibility of Dublin Core was so crucial to our efforts, we chose not to use CORC to catalog exhibits with

FIGURE 2. CREATOR fields for the exhibit, "The Lot Project: contributing to mobility." Highlighted in gray are the group of fields describing corporate authors for the project, including role and geographic location.

DC.Element	Scheme	Element Content
DC.Title		The Lot Project
DC.title.subTitle		contributing to mobility
DC.creator.personalName.1		Bitter, Sabine
DC.creator.personalName.role.1		Artist, Author
DC.creator.corporateName.1		Black Audio Film Collective
DC.creator.corporateName.Address.1		London
DC.creator.corporateName.role.1		Artist
DC.creator.corporateName.2		Sulikowski, Ulrike Davis
DC.creator.personalName.role.2		Artist, Author
DC.creator.personalName.3		Weber, Helmut
DC.creator.personalName.role.3		Artist, Author
DC.creator.personalName.4		Goellner, Toni
DC.creator.personalName.role.4		Artist
DC.creator.corporateName.2		IOOA, Interim Office of Architecture
DC.creator.corporateName.Address.2		San Francisco
DC.creator.corporateName.role.2		Artist
DC.creator.personalName.5		Meister, Juerg
DC.creator.personalName.role.5		Artist
DC.creator.personalName.6		Paris, Heidi
DC.creator.personalName.role.6		Artist
DC.creator.personalName.7		Reisinger, Heinz
DC.creator.personalName.role.7		Artist
DC.creator.personalName.8		Rollig, Stella
DC.creator.personalName.role.8		Author
DC.creator.personalName.9		Weber, Helmut
DC.creator.personalName.role.9		Artist

numerous artists and bodies, such as *The Lot Project*. Nowhere does the CORC Dublin Core view specify the unique relationships of one creator to another. While the 1999 Crosswalk from Dublin Core/MARC/GILS[8] allows the extension *.role* for both CONTRIBUTOR and CREATOR fields, CORC does not include this as an option. Rebecca Guenther, in *Dublin Core Qualifiers/Substructure*, makes the argument that this role is not needed because all names, regardless of their type, are searchable in the same file and that the Library of Congress dropped the use of "role" in such MARC fields years ago. Nevertheless, we felt it critical to include each contributor's name, role, and affiliation in our records.

Further, for a single exhibit including more than one distinct piece, CORC's Dublin Core/MARC mapping prevented us from maintaining the connection between multiple artists and multiple titles that we were able to create using an extended Dublin Core or MARC format. For example, for the exhibit "Transition," we made traditional author/title analytic entries for each of three artworks in the CORC MARC view:

700 12 Nettles, Bea, $d 1946- . $t Moonsisters;

700 12 Kovac. Tom. $t Journey;

700 12 Krepp, Sarah. $t White Noise.

When mapped into the Dublin Core view in CORC, the subfields were split off into variant title entries.

While Dublin Core's minimalist structure, as it is configured in CORC, may not affect access, it ignores the relationships within a major digital art gallery that one would hope to discover right up front. Our experience with the *@art gallery* archive exhibits suggests that, in theory, Dublin Core is adequate for describing these exhibits. It was also satisfactory for constructing complex access points that include creators' names, roles, titles, and affiliations. We were disappointed, however, with the restrictions placed on us by the implementation of Dublin Core in CORC and, to some extent, with the way the Dublin Core/MARC crosswalk maps data between the two views.

CAN THE DUBLIN CORE ADEQUATELY REPRESENT THE DYNAMIC RELATIONSHIPS BETWEEN PIECES, EXHIBITS AND THE GALLERY AS A WHOLE?

Digital art is not a linear medium like a book. Finding citations and bibliographies in a book is predictable. Digital art also often contains links to important outside sources; however, the location of these citations within a piece is not predictable and depends largely on a user's navigational choices. Turning to the *@art gallery* our challenge was to highlight these important links and citations (Figure 3).

The RELATION element in Dublin Core may be used to indicate a reference to a related resource, preferably "by means of a string or number conforming to a formal identification system."[9] The Arts and Humanities Data Service suggests using the extension "IsMemberOf" to indicate a formal (rather than a physical or historical) relationship to another resource.[10] This extension could be used to indicate the connection of the exhibits within the *@art gallery* archive to the gallery itself.

In addition to their formal relationship to the *@art gallery* archive, several

FIGURE 3. First navigation page from "Silence" by Stephanie Cunningham. The arrows indicate the multiple directions a user can choose to go in the exhibit. In addition, each direction presents its own navigational opportunities within. A user may never see key names and links depending on their navigational choices.

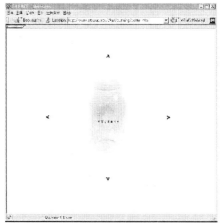

exhibits also maintained a similar, formal relationship to another institution. Steve Goldberg's exhibit, "Raised by Wolves,"[11] has a home in the *@art gallery* archive, but includes an important link to the San Francisco Museum of Modern Art, where a parallel exhibition of "Raised by Wolves" adds context to the *@art gallery*'s exhibit. What kind of relationship does this represent? While each of the archived exhibits may be considered "Members Of" the archive, how should the relationship of parallel exhibits be indicated? We considered briefly the use of "SiblingOf" to describe that relationship. However, according to the Arts and Humanities Data Service, the use of "SiblingOf" should refer to resources "hierarchically adjacent to the resource to which this RELATION points, and is part of the same collection."[12] The parallel exhibit doesn't belong to the same collection, so its relationship remains undefined. How many relationships is it adequate to document in an environment like the Web, where these relationships are liable to multiply beyond manageability?

The RELATION field in Dublin Core is probably adequate to represent the dynamic relationships between pieces, exhibits, and the gallery as a whole. However, making effective use of the RELATION element would require careful analysis, and guidelines to apply it to digital art exhibits could be laborious to set up and maintain. Ultimately, we chose not to use the RELATION field for each and every part of the exhibit, but it is clear that this was a decision based not on a confident assessment of the capabilities of the RELATION field, but rather on a lack of guidance in intellectual terms as to what such a field represents in a digital environment. We recognize, though, that the RELATION field is one of the most difficult to define, as it deals most closely with the tangled aspect of the Web.

CAN THE DUBLIN CORE ADEQUATELY DOCUMENT THE TOOLS NEEDED TO ACCESS AND ACTIVATE DIGITAL ART?

Especially in the case of digital art, detailing equipment requirements as well as indicating the "materials" used to create a work are central for accessing, activating, and preserving the pieces. Many pieces can only be viewed using the latest versions of a Web browser; most use some kind of application such as Macromedia Shockwave; and many suggest screen sizes and monitor settings for the best experience of the work. Equipment requirements are necessary not only to gain the optimum experience of the piece, but also to give the artist some semblance of control over the environment in which the work is viewed.

While one might not expect these elements to be important to a search query, it is possible to imagine that, as production of this sort of work increases, users may become interested in how artists use certain applications, in much the same way that art historians investigate the use of a certain medium over a period of time. Already, searchers use terms such as MP3 to find music in that format on the Web. Equipment requirements should be considered an access point as well as important preservation documentation.

Dublin Core's FORMAT field is defined, in Version 1.1, as the proper repository for "the physical or digital manifestation of the resource . . . FORMAT may be used to determine the software, hardware or other equipment needed to display or operate the resource." The Dublin Core Metadata Initiative's recommended best practice is to select a value from a list, such as the list of *Internet Media Types*.[13] By repeating the FORMAT field for each instance of a required hardware or software application, Dublin Core provides a key access point for digital art.[14]

For the sake of effective use and preservation, we feel that it is imperative that the FORMAT field communicates the structural differences between the many building blocks of a digital artwork–in other words, the information that indicates how the digital artwork can be opened, viewed, executed, or manipulated. It is important to note, for example, that a work is encoded in HTML; however, it is also important to record that a work is best viewed with a particular screen size or that the user needs to download a helper application such as QuickTime in order to view it. These are different sets of information. One refers to the language an operating system needs to interpret, the other to actions that must take place on the part of the viewer in order to activate the piece; they should be stored in such a way that they are decipherable from one another. We also feel "how-to" information should be abstracted in the DESCRIPTION field to provide a link to a detailed list of equipment, software and hardware, requirements in the FORMAT field (Figure 4).

While labor-intensive, providing distinct FORMAT, TYPE and DESCRIPTION fields and repeating the FORMAT field to describe various kinds of system requirements and activation information takes full advantage of the Dublin Core metadata scheme. Using such fields to document digital artworks not only provides important information for their activation and preservation, but further anticipates the goal of accessing artworks created using certain applications or equipment.

HOW DO DUBLIN CORE AND CORC DEAL WITH SUBJECT ANALYSIS FOR CONCEPTUAL WORKS OF ART?

Several papers have been written on subject indexing for historical photographs and works of art.[15] The works in the *@art gallery* archive have more of a narrative quality and are less focused, for the most part, on each individual image. Because of the nature of the Web, each work is the sum of its many images.

We found Dublin Core adequate for describing digital art. The challenge

FIGURE 4. A sample record for "Pleasured Spaces." The scheme field has been used to indicate the kind of format described, as detailed in the source of the vocabulary, Internet Media Types (*http://www.isi.edu/in-notes/iana/assignments/media-types/media-types*).

DC.Element	Scheme	Element Content
DC.format.video	Internet Media Types	QuickTime
DC.format.image	Internet Media Types	gif
DC.format.image	Internet Media Types	jpeg
DC.format.sound	Internet Media Types	basic
DC.format.text	Internet Media Types	HTML
DC.type		Exhibit
DC.description		A World Wide Web art exhibit. Requires sound, QuickTime plug-in, and Netscape 2.0 or higher. Also features a ledger with comments sent via email, regarding the exhibit and its subject matter.

here is determining appropriate subject content. One method is to use controlled vocabularies. We elected to use a mix of controlled vocabularies–including the *Library of Congress Subject Headings* (LCSH),[16] the *Art and Architecture Thesaurus* (AAT),[17] and the *Thesaurus for Graphic Materials* (TGM)[18]–as well as keywords from artist's statements or the text of the piece, when the controlled vocabularies proved inadequate. The scheme extension for Dublin Core was important here in providing a field to indicate source of vocabulary.

Subject designations are especially important for conceptual work in order to pull particular digital art documents together with related bibliographic material in an OPAC. For example, the subject headings "Art, Modern-20th Century" from LCSH and "Computer art" from the *Thesaurus of Graphic Materials* are fine for describing the form and genre of the piece, but do nothing to provide context. Take again the example of "Raised by Wolves," which deals with topics such as homelessness, runaways, child abuse and neglect, and outreach. Here the subject field is the primary access point for collating this exhibit with related materials outside the visual arts.

Another method, possible to some extent in CORC and discussed as a possible goal for subject cataloging,[19] is "automatic harvesting." Automatic harvesting extracts keywords from a digital document and, in the case of CORC, uses an algorithm to assign subject headings and classification numbers. Such a method presents some obvious problems for images that have no accompanying text, but because many of the works in the *@art gallery* included text, we decided to try it out in CORC. The primary stumbling block for CORC's automatic harvesting program is that it cannot interpret the abstract uses of text in the works. For example, the CORC harvester program chose the subject terms "Silence" (781.236), "Secondary schools and programs of specific kinds, levels, curricula, focus" (373.2), and "Animated cartoons" (741.58) for Stephanie Cunningham's "Silence" piece.[20] Our subject assignments were "Sexism" (TGM), "Containers" (TGM), and "Plath, Sylvia, 1932–1936"(LCSH), which themselves are inadequate to describe a piece that uses abstract images to explore abstract ideas. Other works could not utilize the harvesting tool, as they contained less than 500 characters on the page we chose to harvest. And lastly, the harvesting tool can only digest one page at a time, rather than assessing the subject matter of an exhibit's multiple pages. The CORC automatic harvesting program is no doubt in a preliminary stage of development, and its use with resources containing very little text may never be possible.

Dublin Core appears to be adequate for encoding subject and genre terms selected from appropriate vocabularies. We did not find the CORC automatic harvesting feature useful for developing subject terms or class numbers for works in the *@art gallery*.

CONCLUSION

This article presents a case study of Dublin Core in theory and in practice, using the works in the *@art gallery* as a basis for study. To help us with Dublin Core in theory, we examined the guidelines from the Arts and Humanities Data Service and information from the Web site of the Dublin Core Metadata Initiative. To examine Dublin Core in practice, we used the CORC implementation of Dublin Core. In summary, we found:

1. The Dublin Core standard is generally adequate for describing *@art gallery* exhibits. Its elements can be extended to provide complex access points that include artists' names, roles, titles and affiliations. However, the CORC implementation of Dublin Core severely restricts the use of qualifiers that are crucial for describing our exhibits;
2. In theory, the Dublin Core RELATION element can represent the dynamic relationships between pieces, exhibits, and the gallery as a whole. In practice, we found the available guidelines for using the RELATION element inadequate for our needs;
3. The Dublin Core FORMAT field should be extended and repeated in order to effectively document the various structural elements of digital artwork and to provide information necessary to activate and view the pieces as well as to provide documentation for digital preservation. In practice, we found it necessary to provide a "how-to" abstract for the user in a DESCRIPTION field as well;
4. Dublin Core, and its implementation in CORC, are adequate for encoding subject and genre terms and keywords, provided they are assigned manually. We did not find the CORC automatic classification/subject analysis feature useful with *@art gallery* works.

The findings of our case study are likely to be useful to others in the art community who are considering using Dublin Core and CORC to describe digital art. As Dublin Core and CORC are further developed, we suggest that those involved in the Dublin Core Metadata Initiative and those who are building and enhancing CORC take our findings into consideration.

NOTES

1. http://www.art.uiuc.edu/@art
2. http://images.library.uiuc.edu
3. "Research Project to Automate Cataloging of Internet Resources Seeks Participants Worldwide," September 28, 1998, *OCLC News Release. http://www.oclc.org/oclc/press/980928.htm*

4. Paul Miller and Daniel Greenstein, Eds. 1997, *Discovering Online Resources Across the Humanities*: *A Practical Implementation of the Dublin Core*. London: UKOLN.

5. http://www.art.uiuc.edu/@art/leonardo/ensdorf/ensdorf.html

6. Rebecca Guenther. *Dublin Core Qualifiers/Substructure.* "Recommendations for Author or Creator." Last updated October 15, 1997. *http://www.loc.gov/marc/dcqualif.htm*. Note: A number of Dublin Core Working Groups are currently in the process of clarifying Dublin Core qualifiers and extensions. A host of links to those discussions can be found at the Dublin Core Metadata Initiative's Website, *DCMI Working Groups–Qualifier Proposal Information*: *http://purl.oclc.org/dc/groups/qualifierlist.html*

7. Stuart Weibel, 1999, "The State of the Dublin Core Initiative, April 1999" *D-Lib Magazine* Vol. 5, *http://www.dlib.org/dlib/april99/04weibel.html*

8. http://lcweb.loc.gov/marc/dccross.html

9. Dublin Core Metadata Element Set, Version 1.1: Reference Description, *http://purl.oclc.org/dc/documents/rec-dces-19990702.htm*

10. Miller and Greenstein, p. 49.

11. *http://www.art.uiuc.edu/@art/rbw/wolves/wolves.html*

12. Miller and Greenstein, p. 49.

13. *http://www.isi.edu/in-notes/iana/assignments/media-types*

14. Dublin Core Metadata Element Set, Version 1.1: Reference Description, *http://purl.oclc.org/dc/documents/rec-dces-19990702.htm*

15. Karen Collins. "Providing Subject Access to Images: A Study of User Queries." *The American Archivist*. Vol. 61 (Spring 1998): 36-55. Shatford Layne, Sara, "Some Issues in the Indexing of Images." *Journal of the American Society for Information Science*. Vol. 45 (September 1994): 585-88.

16. *Library of Congress Subject Headings*. (Washington, D.C.: Library of Congress, Cataloging Distribution Service, 1975-)

17. *Art and Architecture Thesaurus*. Getty Vocabulary Program. *http://shiva.pub.getty.edu/aat_browser/*

18. *Thesaurus for Graphic Materials I and II*. (Washington, D.C.: Library of Congress Prints and Photographs Division, 1995) *http://lcweb.loc.gov/rr/print/tgm1/toc.html* and http://lcweb.loc.gov/rr/print/tgm2/

19. *Subject Data in the Metadata Record*: *Recommendations and Rationale*. A Report from the ALCTS/CCS/SAC/Subcommittee on Metadata and Subject Analysis. July 1999.

20. These subject headings were probably pulled from text that related to the publisher, the University of Illinois, and the phrase animated gif files.

Using the Dublin Core with CORC to Catalog Digital Images of Maps

David Yehling Allen

SUMMARY. This article deals with cataloging digital images of maps using the Dublin Core format in the CORC environment. In spite of the essential simplicity of Dublin Core cataloging, there are a number of unresolved problems in its application to digital images of maps previously published on paper. These problems are described, and suggestions are made concerning the best way to handle them. Examples are provided of Dublin Core cataloging of varying degrees of complexity for images of historical maps. In the long run, cataloging maps using the Dublin Core format in CORC should get easier as improvements are made in the CORC system and "best practice" guides are developed. *[Article copies available for a fee from The Haworth Document Delivery Service: 1-800-342-9678. E-mail address: <getinfo@haworthpressinc.com> Website: <http://www.HaworthPress.com>]*

KEYWORDS. Cartographic materials, cataloging, CORC, digital images, Dublin Core, historical maps, maps, metadata, OCLC, raster images

INTRODUCTION

Dublin Core cataloging and its implementation in the CORC system have the potential to provide a simple way to catalog the thousands of digital images of maps proliferating on the World Wide Web.

David Yehling Allen is Map Librarian at the State University of New York at Stony Brook.

[Haworth co-indexing entry note]: "Using the Dublin Core with CORC to Catalog Digital Images of Maps." Allen, David Yehling. Co-published simultaneously in *Journal of Internet Cataloging* (The Haworth Information Press, an imprint of The Haworth Press, Inc.) Vol. 4, No. 1/2, 2001, pp. 163-177; and: *CORC: New Tools and Possibilities for Cooperative Electronic Resource Description* (ed: Karen Calhoun, and John J. Riemer) The Haworth Information Press, an imprint of The Haworth Press, Inc., 2001, pp. 163-177. Single or multiple copies of this article are available for a fee from The Haworth Document Delivery Service [1-800-342-9678, 9:00 a.m. - 5:00 p.m. (EST). E-mail address: getinfo@haworthpressinc.com].

163

CORC and/or the Dublin Core also have a number of other potential applications for cataloging the full range of cartographic materials (including maps on paper, atlases, aerial photographs, CD-ROMs, and geospatial data files). But the treatment of these materials is more problematic in CORC, as it presently exists, and my own experience is primarily with using CORC to catalog digital images (raster images) of maps originally published on paper.[1] Therefore, this article will focus on that particular application.

This application is not a trivial one. Thousands of historical maps have already been digitized, and more are on the way.[2] The most notable project involving the digitization of historical maps is being carried out by the Geography and Map Division of the Library of Congress.[3] But a wide range of institutions, ranging from research libraries to small genealogical and historical societies, have been putting maps on the Web. There are many reasons why old maps are popular subjects for digitization. Historians, environmentalists, genealogists, educators, map collectors, and urban planners are among their users. Often, these maps are rare, and it frequently requires a trip to a distant archive to view the originals. Thus, there is a demand for these maps, and the technology now exists to convey high quality images of them over the Internet.

Bibliographic control of these digital images is a major problem. Except in the rare cases where individual maps are listed in the metadata headers of Web pages, standard search engines do not pick them up by title and author. Even when they do, Web search engines do not offer the advantages of searching by field. Listservs used by map librarians and others interested in the history of cartography have carried considerable discussion about how to facilitate finding individual maps on the Web. Creating bibliographic records for these maps in the CORC database seems to be the best available solution for this problem, since CORC provides for searching by field and using Boolean operators. Even with its limited holdings, CORC is already the most comprehensive tool for locating maps on the Internet.

In spite of numerous problems, which will be discussed below, creating records for digital images in Dublin Core format is a fairly easy procedure in the CORC system.

CARTOGRAPHIC MATERIALS, THE DUBLIN CORE, AND THE CORC ENVIRONMENT

The CORC project was begun as an experiment, and it is only a little over a year old. It definitely was not born fully grown, like Athena out of the brow of Zeus, and its implementation has presented many difficulties. The problems are gradually being worked out, and by the time CORC goes into production mode around the middle of this year, users should find it much easier to work with.

It is possible to catalog maps in CORC using both MARC 21 and the Dublin Core formats. Most of the records for maps in the CORC database appear to have been originally done in MARC, although they can be viewed in both formats. Not being a cataloger, I have worked with the simpler Dublin Core format. Part of the appeal of the Dublin Core is that it can be used by map librarians who are not catalogers, by paraprofessionals, and by staff at smaller institutions that cannot afford to hire and train a map cataloger.

In theory, it should be much easier for novice catalogers to work with the Dublin Core rather than MARC, but in practice I encountered many difficulties. Most of the problems arise from the newness of both the Dublin Core and CORC, and from the lack of established standards and documentation for working with them. As more librarians gain experience in working with Dublin Core cataloging in CORC, and "best practice" guidelines are established, most of the problems should disappear. Ironically, one source of confusion has been the very simplicity of Dublin Core cataloging. The basic Dublin Core record consists of only fifteen elements, none of which are mandatory, all of which are repeatable, and all of which can be of any length and in any order. Given this situation, it is understandable that there should be some confusion about what goes where, especially when dealing with complex bibliographic records. Progress has been made in defining the content of the fifteen elements, but it is still not always clear how some of them should be applied in specific cases.[4] Guides to best practice have been developed for the basic Dublin Core elements. These are helpful, but none specifically address cartographic materials.[5]

As a result of the Dublin Core Metadata Initiative, more structure was added to the Dublin Core's basic elements through the addition of extensions or "qualifiers." The purpose of some of these qualifiers is still not adequately defined, and not all of them have been implemented in CORC. There is still little documentation to help CORC users figure out how to apply the qualifiers. In the past year, the CORC staff has added to and changed the available qualifiers, which means that records in CORC only a few months old are likely to be cataloged somewhat differently from those done today. Furthermore, the CORC staff has been reluctant to issue rules concerning how CORC should be used–believing that guidelines for applying the Dublin Core should arise from the user community. They have only recently made it mandatory that all records contain a title. In short, the rules for applying the Dublin Core elements and qualifiers are still in flux, and it is often difficult to decide in which field to enter information. By the time this article is published, it is likely that more extensive documentation and guidelines will be available from CORC.

The situation is further complicated for maps by the lack of guidelines from map catalogers themselves. There is no agreement among map librarians as to what constitutes a minimally acceptable bibliographic record for a map, and some of the rules for cataloging complex cartographic materials are still undetermined.[6] Translating existing or emerging standards for cataloging cartographic materials into Dublin Core format is a task that has scarcely begun. To further complicate matters, there is a major unresolved controversy, which will be touched upon below, concerning how digital images should be treated using the Dublin Core. These uncertainties and unresolved problems have made most map librarians reluctant to work with the Dublin Core, at least until some of the dust settles. This situation will doubtless persist until such time as map librarians themselves come to some agreement concerning what is "best practice" and "minimally adequate" Dublin Core cataloging, and how they should be implemented in the CORC environment. Fortunately, here, too, help is at hand. The Cataloging and Classification Committee of the American Library Association's Map and Geography Round Table (MAGERT) has recently instituted a task force to study and make recommendations on the use of the Dublin Core for cartographic materials.[7]

CREATING SIMPLE BIBLIOGRAPHIC RECORDS FOR RASTER IMAGES OF MAPS

In spite of the nebulosities described above, digital images of paper maps are usually fairly easy to catalog in Dublin Core format. For those bold spirits who don't mind cataloging in an environment where all the rules have not been laid down, I can provide some suggestions. These may be of some use until more detailed and authoritative guidelines are developed.

My suggestions reflect my own background, which involves considerable experience as a creator of computerized bibliographies of maps, but not as a cataloger. I am mainly concerned about how CORC and the Dublin Core can help map librarians with limited time and cataloging expertise. As a librarian, I nonetheless recognize the value of uniform cataloging and urge that CORC records be modeled as closely as possible on standard MARC and AACR2. This commonality will facilitate the use of Dublin Core and MARC on the same platform, ensure that searches for records in automated systems will retrieve the maximum number of relevant records, and make it easier to upgrade Dublin Core to full MARC cataloging.

Because of the flexibility of the Dublin Core, records for maps in CORC can range from the very simple to the very complex. Creating a simple record is fairly intuitive for librarians, since most of the basic fields (such as Creator, Title, Publisher, and Description) resemble those in many familiar bibliographic formats, and there are no numeric tags to worry about. The following record is fairly typical of those I have been creating:

CORC: 201093 *Created:* YSM 1999-07-08
Status: Complete *System:* OCL 1999-10-27

Title	A mapp of New England
Identifier.URL	http://www.sunysb.edu/libmap/img022.jpg
Publisher	Seller
Publisher.Place	London
Coverage.Time	1675
Creator.PersonalName	Seller, John
Date.Issued	1998
Description.Physical	col. map; 45 x 55 cm.
Description.Note	Scale 1:950,400
Description.Summary	John Seller's 1675 map of New England and New York.
Format.MIME	image/JPEG (593 kb)
Language	en
Rights	Contact John Carter Brown Library.
Relation.IsPartOf	Originally published in his Atlas Maritimus.
Relation.Note	Digital image of map held by the John Carter Brown Library. Image derived from Kodak Photo CD using slide purchased from John Carter Brown Library.
Subject.Geographic	New England--Maps--Early works to 1800
Subject.Geographic	New York (State)--Maps--Early works to 1800

Those who undertake to create such records should try to follow standard cataloging conventions as much as possible. Names should be entered last name first; standard library practice should be followed for capitalization of titles; maps should be measured in centimeters (top to bottom, then left to right). Scale (if used) should be entered as a ratio. Name authority control should be used wherever possible (the CORC system includes name and subject authority information).

There is no agreement concerning what constitutes the minimum number of fields in an acceptable Dublin Core record for a map. Creator (author), title, and date of publication would seem to be the only absolutely essential descriptive fields. When available, publisher and place of publication would also be included by most catalogers. I consider the physical description to be important. Some would consider scale or even bounding coordinates to be essential. Most libraries would want to put some sort of classification number in their records. Although maps can often be located using title or subject keywords, standardized subject access is highly desirable. For consistency of retrieval in databases with MARC records, the use of LC subject headings is strongly recommended. As alternative sources of geographic names, digital gazetteers, such as *The Getty Thesaurus of Geographic Names* or the U.S. government's *Geographic Names Information System (GNIS),* might be used.[8]

The only other fields that should be included in a basic Dublin Core record for a digital image of a map are those needed to locate and use the images. These would, of course, include the URL for the resource. It is useful to indicate what type of file the record is pointing to (html, GIF, JPEG, etc.), and give an indication of the file size. Something should also be put in the "Rights" field concerning whom to contact about use of the image. In this record, the "Relation.Note" field is used to describe the chain of transformations between the original map and the image that appears on the Web. This usage is not well established, but seems reasonable to me.

Many map catalogers would urge the inclusion of such information as projection, scale, and geographic coordinates in all records. But the creation of high-level cataloging requires a much greater investment in training and staff time, and librarians have to ask themselves whether the improvement in access made possible through the creation of such records justifies the additional time and expense. The same can be said concerning the inclusion of detailed metadata on how an image was created. Information of this type includes dynamic range, color look-up tables, and characteristics of original image capture (such as scanning process, light source, and source image). Image creation information may be useful for some, but how essential is it for most users of simple GIF and JPEG images? For those interested in high-level cataloging in Dublin Core, the Library of Congress has prepared a Dublin Core-MARC crosswalk. The latest revision of this crosswalk includes many of the qualifiers for the Dublin Core.[9]

Note the handling of the date of publication in the above record. The date of original publication is placed under "Coverage.Time," which is the practice recommended for the Dublin Core. If the information had been available, the date of publication of the digital image would have been placed under "Date.Issued." Since that information was not available, "Date.DataGathered" was used. This is not the practice I would like to see adopted for dates. Ideally, I would prefer to see "Date.Issued" reserved for the date of publication of the original; "Coverage.Time" restricted to situations such as a modern map showing Europe at the time of Napoleon; and a new qualifier, such as "Date.Digitized," introduced for the date of creation of the digital image.

Another unusual feature in the above record is the use of the "Subject.Geographic" heading. This is basically an ordinary Library of Congress Subject heading for a geographic place (MARC 651). According to Eric Childress of CORC, this heading is used by the CORC system to make it easier to identify and work with geographic names. Interestingly, the CORC Dublin Core format does not display the new LC hierarchical subject headings (MARC 752) when found in MARC records. According to Mr. Childress, catalogers should consider entering them in the "Coverage.Geographic" field. Childress also recommends entering geographic keywords in the "Coverage.Geographic" field, rather than as ordinary keywords.[10] Clearly, more work needs to be done to standardize and clarify the use of geographic terms in the CORC version of the Dublin Core format.

Also in flux is the identification of cartographic materials by genre as maps, aerial views, etc. The Dublin Core includes an element for document type, and this would seem to be the ideal place for an identification tag or tags for cartographic materials. Unfortunately, "maps" is not recognized as a document type by the Dublin Core community. Library of Congress subject headings include terms like "maps" or "aerial views," but, with the adoption of form/genre cataloging, this will no longer be the case. Map librarians should lobby for the adoption of "maps" as a document type in Dublin Core. If it were used consistently, the word "map" in the "Description.Physical" field might serve the same purpose. Until a standard method of identifying maps is adopted, I would suggest the inclusion of "maps" as a keyword if the term is not used in a subject heading for a record. It is certainly important to have some means of limiting subject searches to maps.

Another serious problem catalogers may encounter is creating records with diacritics and special characters (including the degree sign used in geographic coordinates). As of the date of this writing, special characters have to be entered by placing a code between two vertical bar (pipe) symbols–for example |ds| for degree sign. At present these codes do not display the symbols they represent, and they make searching for words with diacritical characters nearly impossible. These problems are supposed to be fixed "when the CORC database migrates to Unicode," which should have happened by the time this article appears in print.[11]

Last but not least, it should be noted that my treatment of digital images as surrogates of the originals is controversial. There is a major debate within the Dublin Core community about how to catalog materials formatted as digital images. One issue is the extent to which catalogers should treat images as surrogates of the originals (much as microforms or photocopies) and the extent to which each image should be cataloged as an original, unique creation. Assignment of such elements as "Creator," "Publisher," and "Date" is affected by how one regards this issue. One school of thought would assign all of these elements to the digital product and relegate information about the original to the "Source" element (which can be used for information about the resource from which the digital resource is derived), or to the "Relation.Is FormatOf" field, which is now preferred.[12]

The approach I have outlined above leads to results very similar to existing Library of Congress map cataloging displayed in Dublin Core format. The following is an example of LC cataloging for one of the map images they have placed on the Web. (Keep in mind that the record was originally created in MARC, and that the Dublin Core display is produced by the CORC software.) The record looks much the same as a record for a paper map, with the sole exception of the addition of the "Identifier.URL" field.

CORC: 87   *Created:* DLC   1972-09-06
Status: *System:*   OCL   1999-05-01

Title	Map of New Jersey and Pennsylvania · exhibiting the post offices, post roads, canals, railroads, & c.
Identifier.URL	http://hdl.loc.gov/loc.gmd/g3810.rr002550
Publisher.Place	Washington, D.C.,
Creator.PersonalName	Burr, David H., 1803-1875.
Date.Issued	1839
Description.Physical	col. map · 91 x 124 cm. on 4 sheets 48 x 63 cm.
Description	Relief shown by hachures.
Description.Summary	Detailed map showing relief by hachures, drainage, township and county boundaries, cities and towns, canals, roads, and railroads. [From published bibliography].
Language	english
Relation.IsReferencedBy	LC Railroad maps,
Subject.LCC	G3810 1839
Subject.Geographic	New Jersey · Maps.
Subject.Geographic	Pennsylvania · Maps.
Subject.LCSH	Railroads · New Jersey · Maps.
Subject.LCSH	Railroads · Pennsylvania · Maps.
Subject.LCSH	Postal service · New Jersey · Maps.
Subject.LCSH	Postal service · Pennsylvania · Maps.
Subject.LCSH	Post roads · New Jersey · Maps.
Subject.LCSH	Post roads · Pennsylvania · Maps.
Subject.LCSH	Canals · New Jersey · Maps.
Subject.LCSH	Canals · Pennsylvania · Maps.

Note that the field for map scale, which displays in the MARC version of this record, is not mapped to the Dublin Core version. Scale is included along with latitude-longitude coordinates in the MARC 255 field. The coordinates are mapped to the Dublin Core "Coverage.Geographic" field, but, at present, there is no explicit home for scale. In my own work, I include scale in a descriptive note. It should also be observed that the "Date.Issued" field in the above record corresponds to the date of publication of the original map, as is the case with all the Library of Congress records for historical maps that I have seen in CORC. This record also is missing the "Format.MIME" field, which is not usually included in LC records for historical maps, but which I use to indicate file type and size.

Records in CORC for cartographic images can be much simpler than either of the above examples. The following is an example of a record that the present author created from a record retrieved from the Web.

CORC: 208856   *Created:* YSM 1999-10-26
Status: Complete   *Modified:* YSM 1999-11-11

Title	Chief points of interest in upper Manhattan
Description.Summary	Black and white tourist map (1920).
Coverage.Time	1920
Date.DataGathered	1999-10-26
Format.MIME	image/JPEG (429K)
Identifier.URL	htttp://www.lib.utexas.edu/Libs/PCL/Map_collection/ historical/Manhattan_upper_1920.jpg
Publisher.Name	Automobile Blue Book
Subject.Geographic	New York (N.Y.)--Maps

Although the above record would benefit from bibliographic enrichment, it was the best that could be done using the information available on the Web and without extensive research. I would submit that a simple record like this provides enough information for most researchers to locate the map. It is certainly better than nothing.

HIGH-LEVEL CATALOGING IN DUBLIN CORE FORMAT

Records in CORC can be much more elaborate than those shown above. Here is a record containing most of the information that would be found in a standard MARC record for a paper map, along with a good deal of image metadata. This record is for a map that can no longer be found on the Web. It is for the image of a 1936 facsimile of a map originally published in 1780. Recently, it was replaced at the University of Connecticut site by a higher quality image of the original map. Nonetheless, I will continue to use this example because it illustrates, in a single record, several interesting problems that catalogers of map images may encounter. This record also serves as a reminder of another problem–that maps on the Web are considerably more ephemeral than maps on paper. This, in turn, raises questions about how much time and effort should be spent on creating bibliographic records for such short-lived creations.

CORC: 202432   *Created:* YSM 1999-08-05
Status: Complete   *System:* OCL 1999-10-27

Title	Connecticut and parts adjacent by Bernard Romans.
Title.Alternative	Connecticut at the time of the ratification of the Constitution.
Identifier.URL	http://magic.lib.uconn.edu/exhibits/ scannedmaps/ct1777.html

Publisher	U.S. Geological Survey
Publisher.Place	[Washington, D.C.?]
Contributor.PersonalName	Klockoff, H.
Contributor.CorporateName	United States. Constitutional Sesquicentennial Commission Geological Survey (U.S.)
Coverage.Geographic	W 73°40'--W 71°46'/N 42°10'--N 40°58
Coverage.Time	1777
Creator.PersonalName	Romans, Bernard, ca. 1720-ca. 1784.
Date.Issued	1937
Date.DataGathered	1999-08-05
Description.Edition/Version	Reprint of map published in 1780 by Covens and Mortier, Amsterdam. Originally published in Norwich, Conn., 1777.
Description.Physical	Scale [ca. 1:500,000]
Description.Note	1 map : col. ; 46 x 52 cm.
Description.Note	UCONN MAGIC: Connecticut Scanned Historical Maps
Description.Note	Relief shown pictorially.
Description.Note	Shows counties, towns, rivers, and post roads.
Description.Note	LC copy annotated in pencil: By Bernard Romans, 1777.
Description.Note	In upper border : Connecticut at the time of the ratification of the Constitution, from a 1780 original in the Library of Congress at Washington, issued by the United States Constitution Sesquicentennial Commission.
Description.Note	Scanned from the copy.
Description.Note	Image: 28.86111 inches high (2,078 pixels) 27.48611 inches wide (1,979 pixels) X dpi: 72 Y dpi: 72 Size in memory: 11,731,944 bytes. Original file size: 923,647 bytes on disk JPEG Compression 24-bit RGB Color
Description.Summary	Scanned image of a facsimile of Bernard Romans map of Connecticut and Long Island originally published in 1780.
Format.MIME	text/html
Language	en
Rights.Access	Contact Map Collection, University of Connecticut.
Rights.URL	http://magic.lib.uconn.edu
Subject.Keyword	Finley; Connecticut; history; map; MAGIC; Map And Geographic Information Center; UCONN; University of Connecticut; GIS; Graphic Information System; Geo-Spatial; Geography; Mapping; ArcInfo; MapInfo
Subject.Geographic	Connecticut -- Administrative and political divisions -- Maps -- Early works to 1800.
Subject.Geographic	Connecticut -- Maps -- Early works to 1800.
Subject.Geographic	Long Island (N.Y.) -- Maps -- Early works to 1800.

The above record illustrates one way a very complete cataloging record in Dublin Core format could be presented in CORC, although the choice of fields for some of the information is debatable. It also illustrates some of the problems that come up in assigning traditional author, publisher, and date information to a digital image of a map, which is itself a copy of a 1937 facsimile of an early map published in 1780 (which, is turn, a reprint of a map published in 1777). There is no obvious "best" way of handling these relationships. The assumption followed here is, again, that the researcher is most likely going to be interested in information about the original map, and I have relied on a series of notes to explain the complex chain of relationships between the image and its predecessors. Note also the use of keywords (derived from the metadata header of the Web version of this record at the University of Connecticut). The keywords are used in addition to conventional geographic subject headings. According to recommended Dublin Core practice, it is preferred that each keyword be entered in a separate field, but stringing them together separated by semicolons, as is done here, is acceptable.

The inability of the present version of CORC to provide holdings information is not a serious drawback for images on the Web, since every image is in some ways unique. Each record will have a different URL, and, probably, different images of a map will be scanned at varying resolutions or differ in other ways. There may also be multiple images of a map–with some of them being details. Records for at least two different images of the Romans map discussed above can be found in the CORC database, and multiple records can be found there for several other historical maps with more than one image on the Web.

PATHFINDERS FOR MAPS

A word should be said about the use of "pathfinders" in the context of this discussion of records for digital images of maps. CORC has the ability to create "dynamic pathfinders" on any subject, including maps.[13] These are pages of links to materials on the Web and elsewhere and can be based on predefined searches. The pathfinders can be automatically updated by CORC when new records matching predefined search criteria are added to the database. As an experiment, I created a simple pathfinder for all of the New York State Maps in CORC (pathfinder no. 114). The pathfinder creation process still needs perfecting. As of this writing, I find that some records meeting the criteria of a search are not picked up by the software used for creating pathfinders, and I have also encountered occasional problems with the software creating duplicate records. For these reasons, and because many of the links of the URLs for materials in the database have changed, I found it necessary to download my pathfinder as an HTML document and edit it before making it widely available.[14] In spite of the problems, pathfinders are potentially useful as a way to allow novice users to find maps on a particular region or subject.

One peculiarity of pathfinders should be mentioned. If you want a description of a resource included with each link, the information has to be entered in a field entitled "Description.Summary." This limits the possibilities for creating annotated pathfinders from existing records, although I understand that it will soon be possible to choose from a wider range of fields to use for automatically annotating pathfinder records.

PROBLEMS AND POSSIBLE SOLUTIONS

Although there is much to be said for CORC as a tool for creating and retrieving bibliographic records for images of maps on the Internet, it could be improved. A minor problem is the inability of its search engine to select from the database maps that are actually available on the Internet. A search for maps of a particular subject will indiscriminately retrieve records for both paper maps and Internet resources. This is an annoyance if you are looking for a list of links that you can actually click on and view. This problem could be easily solved by making it possible to exclude from a search records that do not have a URL. I understand that this feature will be implemented when the CORC database is merged into OCLC.[15]

Another problem for CORC users is created by the ephemerality of resources on the Internet. Some of this is unavoidable, but it is frustrating to create records for materials that cease to exist after a few months. Fortunately, most people who put up maps on the Web seem to keep them there more or less indefinitely. More serious is the problem caused by changing URLs, which quickly make many links from CORC obsolete. OCLC has advocated the use of Persistent Uniform Resource Locators (PURLs) to solve this problem, and I heartily endorse the idea.[16] The CORC staff is also investigating ways to automatically identify broken URLs, and, possibly, to correct the addresses of URLs that have changed.

There are also some fundamental problems with CORC as a retrieval tool for historical maps, although most of them are shared with other software used for retrieving maps. Researchers looking for cartographic materials are likely to be concerned with two things: retrieving maps of a specific geographic area and being able to retrieve materials by date of coverage. CORC has significant weaknesses in both of these areas.

Most map searches are usually for coverage of a specific place. The lack of a standardized geographic thesaurus in CORC makes search results less consistent than they would be if a uniform scheme, such as LC subject headings, were used. Nonetheless, the geographic subject headings used by the Library of Congress are little more than keywords, which are usually found in the title of a map. Thus, the lack of authority control is only a moderate drawback for keyword searching.

A broader problem, which CORC does nothing to address, is the inadequacy of both keyword and subject searching as a means of retrieving maps of a specific area. A researcher studying, say, a particular town, may want to look at many items that do not include the town name in either the title or the subject fields–these commonly include county maps, topographic maps, and aerial photographs. To solve this problem, map librarians have fought long and hard for the inclusion of geographic coordinates (longitude and latitude) in bibliographic records. As mentioned above, CORC has responded to this need by designating a specific field (Coverage.Geographic) for coordinates. But CORC does not as yet include any means of searching for records that include or fall within a specific set of coordinates. This type of search is best done with a graphical interface in which the user can bring up a list of all of the maps that provide coverage for an area within a box drawn on a computer screen.

Even if CORC eventually provides for a means of searching by coordinates, it still leaves the problem that very few of the records in CORC (or elsewhere) actually contain them. For many institutions, it simply requires too much expertise or time for catalogers to include them. The solution for providing improved geographic access may come through the development of a geographic thesaurus linked to coordinates for each place name. Such a system, which is under development as part of the Alexandria Digital Library Project, could automatically retrieve the coordinates for all of the place names located through a search of a database such as CORC and then retrieve additional records covering the same geographic area. The success of such a system would, of course, depend on having the place names entered in a form it could recognize–which brings us back to the problem of authority control.[17]

The related problem of finding maps showing an area at a particular time should be easier to deal with. If both the "Coverage.Time" field and "Date.Issued" fields could be searched at the same time and by ranges of dates, the problem would be solved. This would involve a relatively simple change in the CORC software. Of course, it would help if all of the records of digital images of historical maps had the date of publication in the same field. At present, few records use the recently instituted "Coverage.Time" field, and it may well be that most libraries will continue to place the date of publication of the original paper map in the "Date.Issued" field.

CONCLUSION

The CORC project is in its infancy, and it is too early to tell what it may look like as it evolves and is integrated into the OCLC database. It is certainly having its full share of growing pains. From the point of view of a map librarian, CORC holds out most promise as a means of keeping track of digital images of maps on the Internet. Since CORC uses a Web browser and can provide links directly to digital resources, it stands out in this area. In spite of many solvable problems, the simplicity of Dublin Core cataloging makes it much more suitable than MARC for the creation of bibliographic records for rapidly multiplying Internet resources in a world in which professional map catalogers do not abound. CORC also has possibilities as a means of cataloging and making available information about paper maps, as well as

FDGC metadata, but its future for these applications seems more uncertain. The Dublin Core may eventually become a widely used international standard for map cataloging, but the future of the Dublin Core is not necessarily dependent on CORC. The eventual success of both the Dublin Core and CORC as means of dealing with cartographic materials is dependent on many things. Chief among these is probably the development of a consensus among map catalogers as to how the Dublin Core should be applied to various types of cartographic materials, and how it should be used by catalogers with varying amounts of time and expertise.

NOTES

1. Raster images are made up of a grid (or raster) of pixels. Such images are typically produced by scanners or digital cameras. Other maps and cartographic data files on the Internet are in vector format. They are usually produced by Geographic Information Systems (GIS) and consist of mathematically defined lines and curves. Information on cataloging vector maps in Dublin Core can be found in Adam Chandler, Dan Foley, and Alaaeldin M. Hafez, "Mapping and Converting Essential Federal Geographic Data Committee (FGDC) Metadata into MARC21 and Dublin Core: Towards an Alternative to the GGDC Clearinghouse" at: <http://eeirc.nwrc.gov/pubs/crosswalk/fgdc-marc-dc.htm>.

2. For an overview of the issues surrounding the digitization of historical maps, see David Yehling Allen, "Creating and Distributing High Resolution Cartographic Images," *RLG DigiNews*, Vol. 2, No. 4 (August 15, 1998). Available at: <http://www.rlg.org/preserv/diginews/diginews2-4.html>. Many of the sites containing images of historical maps are reviewed in Kristen Block, "Old Maps Meet New Technologies in the Digital Classroom," *Mapline*, No. 88/89 (Fall, 1999), 9-15.

3. The Web site for the online map collections at the Library of Congress is at: *<http://lcweb2.loc.gov/ammem/gmdhtml/gmdhome.html>*.

4. The latest interpretation is: Dublin Core Metadata Element Set, Version 1.1: Reference Description <http://Purl.oclc.org/dc/documents/rec-dces-19990702.htm>. "Status of this document: This is a Dublin Core Metadata Initiative Recommendation. Publication as a recommendation signifies that the specifications are stable and are supported for adoption by the Dublin Core community."

5. Guides to best Dublin Core practice include: Consortium for the Computer Interchange of Museum Information, *Guide to Best Practice: Dublin Core* (August, 1999) <http://www.cimi.org/documents/meta_bestprac_final_ann.html>; *Guidelines for Use of Dublin Core in University of Chicago Library Projects, <http://www.lib.uchicago.edu/Annex/TechSvcs/dcguidelines.html>*.

6. For an authoritative guide to cataloging practices for maps and other cartographic materials (including geospatial data), see the newly published *Maps and Other Cartographic Materials*, ed. Paige G. Andrew and Mary Lynette Larsgaard (New York: Haworth Information Press, 1999). This book was also published as a special double issue of *Cataloging & Classification Quarterly* (Vol 27, nos. 1/2 and 3/4).

7. The charge and membership of the task force is posted on the Cataloging and Classification Committee's home page at: <http://www.sunysb.edu/libmap/catcom.

htm>. Reports and other materials from the task force may also appear on this page. These reports and other new developments relating to the application of the Dublin Core to cartographic materials will be linked to or described on MAGERT's frequently revised "Metadata Primer for Map Librarians" at: *<http://www.sunysb.edu/ libmap/metadata.htm>*.

8. The Getty Information Institute's *Thesaurus of Geographic Names* can be found at <http://shiva.pub.getty.edu/tgn_browser/>. The URL for the Geographic Names Information System is <http://mapping.usgs.gov/www/gnis/>.

9. The Library of Congress Dublin Core/MARC/GILS Crosswalk (14 Oct. 1999) is available at: <http://lcweb.loc.gov/marc/dccross.html>.

10. E-mail message from Jonathan Fausey and Eric Childress to the present author (February 11, 2000).

11. The procedures for dealing with diacritical marks are described in the "CORC System Quick Reference" guide (last revision May 14, 1999), 47-49.

12. Many of these issues are summarized in: Weibel, Stuart, and Eric Miller, "Image Description on the Internet: A Summary of the CNI/OCLC Image Metadata Workshop, September 24-25, 1996." *D-Lib Magazine*, January 1997. <http:// www.dlib.org/dlib/january97/oclc/01weibel.html>. At least in the United States, my recommendation that maps and other digital images of materials on paper should be cataloged as surrogates seems to be gaining ground. This approach is recommended by the University of Chicago Guidelines cited above. As will be seen, it is also reflected in the way the Library of Congress has been cataloging its digital images of maps.

13. For information on pathfinders, see "Pathfinder Quick Reference" (last updated November 11, 1999) at the CORC Web site at: <http://corc.oclc.org>.

14. The edited version of my pathfinder can be seen at: <http://www.sunysb.edu/ libmap/nypath1.htm>.

15. E-mail message from Jonathan Fausey and Eric Childress to the present author (February 1, 2000).

16. For information about PURLs, see: <http://purl.oclc.org>.

17. Information about the Alexandria Digital Library Gazetteer Project is available at: <http://www.alexandria.ucsb.edu/gazetteer/>.

Index